Cambridge Elements

Elements in Contemporary Performance Texts
edited by
Fintan Walsh
Birkbeck, University of London
Duška Radosavljević
Royal Central School of Speech and Drama, University of London
Caridad Svich
Rutgers University

ENGLISH PLAY DEVELOPMENT UNDER NEOLIBERALISM, 2000–2022

Lucy Tyler
University of Reading

Shaftesbury Road, Cambridge CB2 8EA, United Kingdom

One Liberty Plaza, 20th Floor, New York, NY 10006, USA

477 Williamstown Road, Port Melbourne, VIC 3207, Australia

314–321, 3rd Floor, Plot 3, Splendor Forum, Jasola District Centre, New Delhi – 110025, India

103 Penang Road, #05–06/07, Visioncrest Commercial, Singapore 238467

Cambridge University Press is part of Cambridge University Press & Assessment, a department of the University of Cambridge.

We share the University's mission to contribute to society through the pursuit of education, learning and research at the highest international levels of excellence.

www.cambridge.org
Information on this title: www.cambridge.org/9781009598712

DOI: 10.1017/9781009411202

© Lucy Tyler 2025

This publication is in copyright. Subject to statutory exception and to the provisions of relevant collective licensing agreements, with the exception of the Creative Commons version the link for which is provided below, no reproduction of any part may take place without the written permission of Cambridge University Press & Assessment.

An online version of this work is published at doi.org/10.1017/9781009411202 under a Creative Commons Open Access license CC-BY-NC 4.0 which permits re-use, distribution and reproduction in any medium for non-commercial purposes providing appropriate credit to the original work is given and any changes made are indicated. To view a copy of this license visit https://creativecommons.org/licenses/by-nc/4.0

When citing this work, please include a reference to the DOI 10.1017/9781009411202

First published 2025

A catalogue record for this publication is available from the British Library

ISBN 978-1-009-59871-2 Hardback
ISBN 978-1-009-41118-9 Paperback
ISSN 2753-2798 (online)
ISSN 2753-278X (print)

Cambridge University Press & Assessment has no responsibility for the persistence or accuracy of URLs for external or third-party internet websites referred to in this publication and does not guarantee that any content on such websites is, or will remain, accurate or appropriate.

English Play Development under Neoliberalism, 2000–2022

Elements in Contemporary Performance Texts

DOI: 10.1017/9781009411202
First published online: March 2025

Lucy Tyler
University of Reading

Author for correspondence: Lucy Tyler, L.S.Tyler@reading.ac.uk

Abstract: *English Play Development under Neoliberalism, 2000–2022* is the first study of the institutionalising of English play development practices in the twenty-first century. It identifies the ways in which support for playwrights and text development increased beneficially during the 1990s and 2000s. It assesses bureaucratic institutional dynamics in key English producing houses as they were surveyed by two reports in 2009, and how these were experienced and transformed in the 2010s. The Element identifies in new play development innovations in the commodification and marketisation of new writing, the bureaucratisation of literary management, the structuring and restructuring of dramaturgy according to Fordist, then post-Fordist, conditions, and the necessity for commissioned artists to operate as neoliberal subjects. It concludes with attention to a liberatory horizon for play development in the English context. This title is also available as Open Access on Cambridge Core.

This Element also has a video abstract: www.cambridge.org/ECTX_Tyler_abstract

Keywords: English theatre, neoliberalism, Marx, UK party politics, national theatre

© Lucy Tyler 2025

ISBNs: 9781009598712 (HB), 9781009411189 (PB), 9781009411202 (OC)
ISSNs: 2753-2798 (online), 2753-278X (print)

Contents

Introduction: Institutionalising English Play Development   1

1 Policing Literary Management in the 2000s   11

2 Dramaturgy Factories in Key English Theatres in the 2010s   23

3 'You Say You Suffer from a Gentle Schizophrenia': Artistic Subjectivity inside English Play Development in the 2010s   36

Conclusion: Dreaming or Drowning? English Play Development Today   50

References   57

Introduction: Institutionalising English Play Development

In 2014, in the foyer of the Lyric Hammersmith Theatre, I encountered a banner that said 'we think art is not a commodity'. The slogan was the third principle of the Secret Theatre Company's six-part manifesto and referred to their principles of practice. It was also an approach to marketing; six performances made in succession were programmed and would tour without the usual copy. The plays' blurbs had been replaced by a series of questions and titles had been replaced with tags – 'Show 1' through to 'Show 6'. When I noticed the banner, however, I had just purchased tickets to the shows on my credit card for £75. It wasn't just the irony of the commodity exchange that made this encounter memorable – it was the slogan in relation to my personal debt, my personal debt in relation to the cost-of-living crisis, the government austerity programme, its reductions in welfare spending, local funding, the library cuts and closures, the food banks, immigration sanctions, 'big strategic moves' such as National Health Service (NHS) healthcare provision falling five times more per person in Blackpool than in Surrey. Theatre's infinite jest was having an actual laugh. What would it be to remain under this slogan for a decade, drag the confused outrage into theatre production after production, into theatre class after class? It is to appreciate that in England, in the development of a new performance in the twenty-first century, everyone involved is wondering, privately, at what mast they can fly that flag.

My career has been in what Steve Waters (in Luckhurst 2006: 213) and Lyn Gardner (2006) refer to as the 'culture of play development'. In the mid 2000s, when I was an undergraduate creative writing and English literature student, a few theatres with 'new writing' repertoires took interest in my playwriting. Later, I did an MPhil in playwriting studies at the University of Birmingham and received a handful of engagements and commissions from English and American theatres and companies, including Hampstead Theatre, Soho Theatre, and Paines Plough Theatre Company in London; Origin Theater in New York; and Georgetown Theater Company. Later, I undertook reading placements at theatres and script services including Script in Birmingham and Tobacco Factory Theatres in Bristol. A group of friends and I established a theatre company and, in 2010, I started a post teaching playwriting at the University of Gloucestershire. There, I introduced students to the culture of play development, arranging live briefs and commissions with the Everyman Theatre, Cheltenham, and Dreamshed Theatre Company. Commencing wage labour in higher education was slightly lost on me in my naiveté. Like English play development, I lacked an understanding of the (experientially toxic) culture into which I entered and remained.

During the same period, I was politically active, engaged in organising, agitating, and grassroots community building. I was involved with Solidarity Federation (SolFed) and Industrial Workers of the World (IWW). During my annual leave, actions took me on journeys across Europe to explore and engage with sites of historic and ongoing resistance and revolution – all of it with 'one of this country's most important left-wing fiction writers', D. D. Jonston, who was committed to 'bringing light to a dark world' (Barbican Press 2021). Once or twice a week, we would attend study groups with comrades to analyse political economic texts. Meanwhile, I wrote plays about Soviet cells and anarchist Spanish Civil War organisations, and I refused my vote in UK party political elections. The University and College Union was a means through which some of these ideas could meet my new wage labour. I struggled, however, to find intersections between the culture of the academy and English play development and the kind of class consciousness that held my attention in my twenties. In London, the people and places and cultures I sought out politically seemed worlds apart from the commodified theatre I also (somewhat secretively) consumed.

In 2016, I took up a new position at the University of Reading, where, in my role as Associate Professor of Performance Practices, I continue to create an interface between play development and the academy. For instance, alongside John Luther, Artistic Director of South Street Arts Centre, I organise an Arts Council England–funded project, Work in Progress, that seed-funds and facilitates the play development of emerging and mid-stage artists and companies of national and international acclaim. My experience of the culture of English play development supported this later work, but my politics – other than the humility I felt in receiving public money – did not. As time went on, I became less and less involved in political activity and more and more involved in playmaking. I remained amazed, however, by the liberal consensus I found in the culture of English play development. People there, I felt, were friendly, mellow, and repetitively but pleasantly vociferous about two things: Tory governance and identity politics. If there was ever an attempt to interject further socio-historical political-economic thought, however, it would be one step too far: an abrupt contradiction to the gentle, somnambulistic vibe and a bit rude. The critique of the culture of English play development in this Element, however, rudely eschews concerns about middle-class manners and the solipsistic identitarian pathologies that occupy many English theatre makers, to advance instead a class-conscious critique with the discourses, atmospheres, and angers of the radical left.

In my twenties, I assumed that 'play development' referred simply to an exquisite solitary state: a closed theatrical phase in which the playmaker generates raw material and early strategies for text or performance at home or in studios. I imagined all playwrights as gentle souls weeping about the state of things. When I entered the industry, however, I saw that play development was not an isolated preliminary activity. Play development, I would understand, was the sometimes literal space of 'literary management' departments staffed with 'literary managers', 'literary associates', 'readers', and later 'dramaturgs'. It was also a set of meetings undertaken between these roles and playmakers in front-of-house coffee shops, then studios. It was also the somewhat trippy time–space matrix in which playmakers were suspended (or not) when 'on attachment'.

Play development resourcing such as I experienced in the early 2000s had been formalised only in the preceding decade; in the 1990s, English play development as an activity in buildings started to increase. As Jacqueline Bolton (2012) finds, 'in addition to the proliferation of companies who regarded new writing as a core activity, very few producing houses could now exclude it' (219). A field of institutionalised 'literary management' emerged, undertaken at first by what Aleks Sierz (2011) calls 'the big six' new writing theatres: the Traverse in Edinburgh, Live Theatre in Newcastle, and the Royal Court, the Bush, Hampstead, and Soho in London (29). The Royal Court's Young Writers' Programme (as observed by Bolton 2012; Love 2015; Holden 2017) was a key model for other buildings and companies inclined to expand their writerly offering. In the 2000s, as Catherine Love (2015) puts it, there was 'a surge of interest and investment in the developing of new plays by British theatres and companies' (319–320). English play development continued to be instated at English theatres until it might be defined according to what Pierre Bourdieu (1993) describes as a 'field of cultural production'. This field comprises a space of '*relational* thinking' within arts and literary production (29 (original emphasis)). By 2019, play development continued to be advertised as a central activity at the majority of the twenty-nine theatres Sierz (2011) noted as engaging in play development practices in 2011 (32–37).

As a field of cultural production, play development today has an artistic and institutional vocabulary that it takes time to learn. For example, in artistic terms, it is often used interchangeably with 'research and development' ('r&d'). In a theatre building with a new writing repertoire, play development activity is usually undertaken by theatres' literary management strands. For Sue Healy (2022), literary manager of London's Finborough Theatre, the central role of literary management in Ireland and Britain is writer development (5). 'Writer development' and 'play development' are subtly differentiated by the significant economic differences the terms conceal; the latter might refer to plays by an established playwright which a theatre may commission, whereas the former suggests a broader concern with supporting a larger number of would-be or emerging playwrights in honing their craft. In addition to their pseudo-left-wing stance, play development spheres in England are often culturally conjured as anarchistic 'free states' – the last bastions in an otherwise commodified world (e.g. 'we think art is not a commodity'). In this Element, I submit to you the opposite: that these spaces are entirely – devotionally – determined by the political-economic status quo.

By the mid 1990s, play development was becoming increasingly standardised in a valorising process predicated on meeting the consumer demand for new writing's continued exchange value. Play development had become a regulated process, or, to use Marx's (1990 [1867]) term, development now had 'a socially necessary labour time' (129). Scholars working on English theatrical modes of production were already attuned to this. As Bolton (2012) notes, new writing programmes advocated 'conventional principles of drama' that resulted in 'a raft of new plays [that] proved indicative of characteristics that would become familiar as the decade progressed' (217). Moreover, play development had also selected its ideal labour power: young and often first-time playwrights. For Bolton, this was observable most in 'the Royal Court's "strategic and purposeful" targeting of commercially unknown playwrights' (217). The ideal labour power of play development 'encouraged, moreover, a widespread shift in theatres' priorities from new *writing* to new *writers*' (217; emphasis original). At the end of the 1990s, play development practices had revealed their potential as a commodifying process that could effectively valorise plays *and* playwrights (see also Inchley 2015). The economies of scale generated in play development structures translated effectively to subsequent stages of production. As Bolton notes, 'the sheer number of new plays, produced in shorter runs of only two weeks, itself indicated revised attitudes towards the debut play as a cultural event' (217). As Literary Manager Jack Bradley attested, 'the policy was "stack 'em high, sell 'em cheap"' (217).

By the 2000s, English play development was accelerating into, to coin David Harvey (2006), an 'uneven geographical development' across England. The number of theatres engaging with development practices had expanded into a network of nearly thirty building-based theatres, the majority of which were in London. As Sierz (2011) notes, this 'meant new buildings, new staffing levels and new regulations' (30). Arts Council England has produced a range of studies relating to play development at subsidised theatres in England during this period. Emma Dunton, Roger Nelson, and Hetty Shand's *New Writing in Theatre 2003–08: An Assessment of New Writing within Smaller Scale Theatre in England* (Arts Council England 2009c), for example, explores a sample of organisations engaged in play development. The same authors' *Writ Large: New Writing on the British Stage 2003–2009* (Arts Council England 2009b) offers a data set on the most statistically significant producers of new writing between 2003 and 2008. According to their report, these theatres were West Yorkshire Playhouse (now Leeds Playhouse) (5.6%), Plymouth Drum (7.7%), the Birmingham Repertory Theatre (8.5%), the Mercury Theatre (4.2%), the Liverpool Everyman (5.1%), the Royal Exchange Theatre (5.2%), the Royal Shakespeare Company (3.1%), the Royal Court (4.9%), and the National Theatre (5.1%). Other theatres (51%) made up the rest of the new writing produced during this period (55).

Two additional Arts Council England reports shed more light on English play development as a mode of capitalist production. In 2000, Arts Council England published two reports arguing that new writing was in decline. Peter Boyden Associates' *The Boyden Report* (Arts Council England 2000a) argued that text-based theatre was failing to attract audiences and advocated a shift of policy that promoted new, collaborative methods of play development (Arts Council England 2009b: 4). The following Arts Council England (2000b) report of the same year, *The Next Stage: Towards a National Policy for Theatre in England*, accepted *The Boyden Report*'s argument, and the three subsequent reports – *National Policy for Theatre in England* (Arts Council England 2000c), *National Policy for Theatre in England* (Arts Council England 2002a), and *Theatre Policy* (Arts Council England 2007) – all encouraged the production of 'new work': 'new ways of working', 'experimental' and 'interdisciplinary practice' (Arts Council England 2009b: 35–36).

'New work' refers to theatrical approaches that do not centre around the playwright and dramatic play text, including performance-based, devised, ensemble, and Live Art approaches. As Rosalind Haslett (2011) defines it, '"new work" tends to occur in non-traditional forms and spaces' whereas '"new writing" is seen to refer to a literary process which takes place in a conventional theatre building' (358). This definition, as I will show, is suggestive of the significance of Arts Council England's stipulation that theatre organisations should embrace new work and, as a consequence, diversify their play development structures. The shifts in mainstream play development to accommodate new work occurred throughout the 2010s, but, as we will see, have posed some challenges. Furthermore, despite Arts Council England's emphasis on the mainstream development of new work during the 2000s, *Writ Large* noted that 'the Art Council's 2003 *Theatre Writing Strategy* promoted initiatives that presumed a traditional relationship between individual freelance writers and producing companies' (Arts Council England 2009b: 36). In other words, play development practices would continue throughout the 2000s to be undertaken on the established terms at new writing theatres, as Love (2015) evidences in her examination at the Royal Court.

Encouraged by Arts Council England in the aforementioned reports (and in the Traverse's case, the now devolved Creative Scotland), producing theatres and companies started to deploy a set of artistic and literary management methods, pioneered at 'the big six', for engaging new playwrights and their work. These working methods, according to the Writers' Guild (2012), a trade union representing professional writers since 1959, comprised script reports and feedback, building and maintaining creative relationships, mentoring, attachments, seed commissions, workshops, rehearsed readings, scratch nights, treatments, pitch sessions, and collaborative development relationships. The economies of play development during the early 2000s were productive; as the authors of *Writ Large* noted, 'in 2001–2, productions of new commissions and other new work represented 67% of the repertoire ..., in 2002–3 66%, in 2003–4 and 2004–5 71%, in 2005–6 70% and in 2006–7 75%' (Arts Council England 2009b: 40).

The rise in commissions may also be due to the major innovation to literary management during this period: the formalisation of the dramaturg's role in English theatre. The introduction of the dramaturg and dramaturgy to English literary management has been assessed by a number of scholars (Turner and Behrndt 2008, 2010; Turner 2009; Luckhurst 2010; MacDonald 2010; Bolton 2011; Radosavljević 2013a; Trencsényi and Cochrane 2014; Trencsényi 2015). While the early 2000s saw an upturn in new commissions, the austerity measures of the 2010s saw a downturn in play development practices, observed in the empirical data collections of play development. In 2014, Fin Kennedy and Helen Campbell Pickford (2013) produced a 'Delphi study' as a follow-up to their report 'In Battalions'. 'In Battalions' offered a 'snap-shot of play development at the start of 2013' (1) and the follow-up Delphi study intended to continue to assess the effects of Arts Council England cuts on those practices.

A final evolution of play development in the 2000s is the field's inducting of 'new work' and playmakers into the commodifying structures of mainstream play development, which previously had been focused on valorising text-based plays and playwrights. Partly spurred on by Arts Council England's aforementioned interventionist decision to remove new writing from its funding priorities and to advance the cause of new work in *The Boyden Report* (Arts Council England 2000a), theatres started to diversify their play development models and, in some cases, organised parallel development structures for new work. Liz Tomlin (2013c) notes that 'the text-based/non-text-based binary revealed itself in the UK theatre industry in the choice that emerging theatre-makers were constrained to make between the development of opportunities offered by "traditional" new writing flagship theatres ... and those offered by the growing proliferation of arts centres' (9–10). The selection between two stratified play development models artificially disaggregated theatre practice and put pressure on artists to define (and thus to commodify) their projects according to these terms.

In the mid 2010s, however, changes occurred in mainstream play development structures. For example, in 2015, the National Theatre combined its studio, which dealt with writers and devisers, with its literary department, which dealt exclusively with writers. Furthermore, a range of regional theatres, such as the West Yorkshire Playhouse (now Leeds Playhouse), became more engaged in pre-production work with companies and ensembles as noted in Section 2 of this Element. Such changes in English play development have had the effect of diversifying the methodologies of traditional new writing theatres, but they have not always been well received. As Radosavljević (2013a) and Love (2015: 122–123) both note, the British Theatre Consortium and Arts Council England found that writers – the traditional consumers of play development – felt threatened by the diversification. As Radosavljević argues, however, 'the gap between new writing and devising was potentially being perpetrated by political and economic rather than aesthetic and methodological factors' (86). What provokes theatre-makers in play development to decry 'we think art is not a commodity' when scholars counter? What are the political and economic factors determining play development in the twenty-first century?

If 'neoliberalism' broadly describes the approach to governing capitalism in the mid-to-late twentieth and early twenty-first centuries, its ideologies obviously determine the state-subsidised English play development. As Harvey (2005) notes, the administrations of Margaret Thatcher (1979–90) and Ronald Reagan (1981–9) played a central role in aligning UK and US statecraft with capital's interests (1). For Bob Jessop (2018), this process was also observable in Australia, Canada, Cyprus, Ireland, Iceland, and New Zealand (1730). Wendy Brown (2015) argues that neoliberalism may not have been formulated as 'a 1980s political rebellion by new Right populists, not as a vision heralded by a specific set of political leaders and economic craftsmen ... but, rather as an "emergence" over the second and third quarters of the twentieth century' (51–52). Brown thus contends that neoliberalism is an inevitable development in the management of capital in the twentieth century. Jessop (2018) refers to its origins as the 'post-war Atlantic Fordist class compromise [in which] at least six neoliberal policies were pursued in order to modify the balance of forces in favour of capital'. These policies can be summarised as follows: (1) liberalisation to promote the free market, (2) deregulation, (3) privatisation, (4) 'reducing the scope for non-market logics', (5) reductions in corporate income tax, and (6) the promotion of the global flow of goods and services. Neoliberalism has not only destroyed 'prior institutional frameworks and powers (even challenging traditional forms of state sovereignty) but also divisions of labour, social relations, welfare provisions, technological mixes' (1729). As Alana Lentin and Gavan Titley (2011) argue, 'life is reduced to economics and everything, including individual action, is judged according to its profitability and "rationality"' (163). In the UK, the historicisation of neoliberalism is often taken as a totality: with its origin story the neoliberal regime shift during the premiership of Margaret Thatcher, or, as Stuart Hall (2011) puts it in the subtitle to his article 'The Neoliberal Revolution', 'Thatcher, Blair, Cameron: The Long March of Neoliberalism Continues' (9). The crisis manufactured by the Tories referred to as 'Brexit' was a significant event in the long march insomuch as it produced a complex reading of the relationality of the historical material moment and English statecraft. For Colin Hay (2018), Brexit was 'a product of the complex interplay of neoliberalising and counter-liberalising tendencies and counter-tendencies and a combination of neoliberal and neo-conservative reflexes. Put like that, it is hardly surprising that it is likely to prove both neoliberalising and de-neoliberalising in terms of its effects' (6). Because of this ambiguity, Brexit does not play a central part in this Element's reading of the interrelationship between neoliberalism and English play development.

Scholarship has already exposed the genesis and persistence of neoliberalism as a totality across cultural forms, especially theatre (e.g. Harvie 2013; Gilbert 2016; Diamond et al. 2017; Ybarra 2017; Greer 2018; Solga 2019). Jen Harvie, for example, focuses on the theatre's response to the iterations of neoliberalism interpreted by the British governance of New Labour (1997–2010), the Conservative–Liberal Democrat coalition (2010–15), and the recently ousted Conservative government (2015–24). By focusing on the UK's economic context, Britain is not seen to have priority over any other geographical centre for neoliberalism, but rather because the neoliberal order was first assembled as a coherent package in Britain and therefore state-subsidised English theatre making during this period arises from specific material conditions. The features of neoliberalism that will be most familiar to the English public between 2000 and 2022 are its austerity, the creep of bureaucracy into public services, the stealth restructuring of life and work activity according to Fordist and post-Fordist principles, the encroachment of entrepreneurialism, and heightened individualism against a backdrop of devastating inequality. It is these conditions of neoliberalism, and their claim on English play development, that this Element attends to.

The most striking feature of neoliberalism is its untameable aggression. Its exclusionary tendencies in England had become so dysregulated that, by the Covid-19 crisis, scores of unnecessary deaths of Black and South Asian people occurred. While social and economic conditions have continued to reveal sharp disparities in living and working standards across the twenty-first century, England also saw successive socially liberal governments each purporting – ironically – an advancement of equality. According to Peter Ratcliffe (2004), 'New Labour administrations since 1997 . . . all espoused the notion of "One Nation" as an inclusive citizenship' (8). The most significant example of Labour's social liberalism manifested in the year preceding Mark Duggan's death, in the 2010 Equality Act. According to the Government, the Equality Act legally 'protects people from discrimination' (Equity Act Guidance 2015). Protected groups now include age, disability, gender reassignment, marriage and civil partnership, race, religion or belief, and sex and sexual orientation. Here we see a tussle between neoliberalism as a geopolitical framework that gives rise to enormous global inequalities and individual statecraft policies that seemingly seek to ameliorate some of its effects. How do the arts – or more specifically English play development – respond? As Liz Tomlin (2014) notes, 'New Labour's social inclusion agenda . . . was hugely significant in shaping arts policy' (4). In 2011, under the Coalition, Arts Council England launched a new policy document based on the Equality Act entitled *The Creative Case for Diversity* (Arts Council England 2011a). *The Creative Case* was a revised approach for diversity in the arts, including theatre, based around resituating many of the protected categories referenced in the Equality Act into the sphere of English artistic production and consumption under the banner of 'diversity'. Matt Hargrave (2015) uses the term 'new diversity' to articulate how '*The Creative Case* indicates a policy shift from diversity as social deficit to diversity as human value' (83). Hargrave continues by stating that 'the report enfolds diversity and equality to the point where they both vanish. Excellence (the new quality) is only apparent if relevant; and relevance is (currently) diversity; so to be excellent one must be diverse and everyone is diverse; and so on, until the criteria collapse on themselves' (85). The criteria of 'diversity' and 'equality' did not so much collapse, but rather became folded into neoliberalism, with new diversity part of the '*new* spirit' of capitalism (Boltanski and Chiapello 2018 [1999] (my emphasis)). This was clear during the pandemic when the material conditions of neoliberalism's inequality inside English theatre were self-evident. Writing for Arts Council England after the death of George Floyd, for example, Darren Henley (2020) notes that 'it is clear that despite our best intentions, we have so far failed to create the systemic, structural changes needed for our sector to be truly diverse'. Henley continues by arguing that some people are 'experiencing prejudice, intolerance and racism when interacting with some cultural organisations' (54). How could this be, given the aforementioned legislation? Arun Kundnani (2021) argues that neoliberalism is now 'haunted by its own failure to universalize its market order; a racial idea of culture is the means by which this anxiety is managed and worked through' (54). By locating the neoliberal imperative for racial constructs in English theatre, Tom Six (2024) refers to a 'racial regime' that privileges whiteness through colonial hierarchies in some of the theatres mentioned herein. It is beyond the scope of this Element to follow Six in attending to neoliberalism's imbrication in any racialised tendencies in the culture of English play development; however, it is possible to nudge towards the invention of new ways of being with new writing and work, new ways of being with each other, and new protocols that foreground artistic agency, relationality, and solidarity. As Denise Espirito Santo and David Gutierrez suggest, in this 'terminal state of an economic model and a global culture that is responsible for millions of infections and deaths worldwide', we can embrace our vulnerability (in Bissell 2022: 33). More than anything, English play development, as it continues through the twenty-first century, requires both expansion of the point of entry and a location of care for those who enter it.

It is the first two decades of the twenty-first century, however, that are the subject of this Element. And while this introduction has aimed to establish a foundation for an in-depth analysis of neoliberalism and English play development across the 2000–22 period, the sections that follow attend to much shorter and more pivotal moments within the wider frame: 2009, then 2014–18. Across each section, I draw attention to how a key feature of neoliberalism impacted on English play development. In Section 1, I attend to the increase in bureaucracy in English play development in 2009, when governments were responding to the financial crisis of 2007–8. In order to do this, I analyse two Arts Council England reports published in 2009 – *Writ Large* and *New Writing in Theatre 2003–08* (the second referred to with the shorthand *The Dunton Report*) – with some analysis of a 2007 evaluation report published by Firebird Theatre about their production of *Dr Faustus*. In Section 2, I explore how neoliberalism's emphasis on the transformation and restructuring of modes of production according to Fordist and post-Fordist logics was undertaken in English play development. I do this by analysing interviews with practitioners I conducted between 2014 and 2018. Section 3 is an examination of the reconstituting of artistic subjectivity according to neoliberal paradigms that uses the same methodology of practitioner interviews. The participatory data on English play development was collected by open-ended questions that went through two institutional review processes. In the conclusion, I take a different approach by discussing what I see as a site of resistance to neoliberalism's insistence on inequalities.

I offer an account of the recent commissioning and play development of Kwame Owusu's *Dreaming and Drowning* (2023) at The Bush, a new writing theatre in London. I note a direct engagement to the global racial reckoning and demand for truth, freedom, redress, and reform that has inspired an unprecedented social movement since the 2020 murder of George Floyd. We can observe how racial healing can be integrated – for the first time – into an English play development model as a means to resist neoliberalism's failure, as Kundani puts it, to universalise its market order. In so doing, I hope to show that, on occasion, neoliberal imperatives can be set aside. Therein, we hold space for non-hierarchical, global, and receptive modes of decentred play development as a future-oriented model. *La Lutte Continue!*

1 Policing Literary Management in the 2000s

As a reader, my memory of triaging unsolicited scripts in English theatres between 2009 and 2012 is vague. I recollect settings on coastal paths in Cornwall, Mars, a play in a mosque in a post-apocalyptic Walsall, a caravette en route to Calais, the tomb of Tutankhamun. The indeterminacy of these narratives is a telling contradiction to my clear memory of real happenings: the peaceful march to demand information about the death of Mark Duggan, for instance, a Black man from Tottenham, north London – who had been shot dead by the police on 4 August 2011. The riots transformed Britain's approach to protest policing. A decade later, the experiment in emergency 'justice' was once again activated by riots following the police killing of another unarmed Black man, and what the home secretary, Priti Patel, called the violent 'thuggery' of those who believed – beautifully – that their embodied challenge to repressive apparati could be both symbolic and direct. For Adam Elliott-Cooper (2011), 'Neoliberalism, through securitisation, resource reallocation, privatisation of space and the de-racialising of language, has made radical Black activism an increasingly difficult endeavour' (4). Or, to quote David Cameron, 'we are making technology work for us' (BBC 2011). On advising literary departments on triaging unsolicited scripts, Healy (2022) notes 'evaluating them takes up a lot of time and you will have to consider ways to *efficiently manage* this' (29 (my emphasis)). In this section, I show how one feature of neoliberalism, its insistence of bureaucratic excess, infiltrated English play development in the 2000s. In particular, I show how the *efficient management* of unsolicited scripts in England in the twenty-first century became an activity determined by an increasingly repressive state apparatus – observed a decade later in the police force, in our education settings, and in the NHS. Here, I argue that there was a rise of new public management in English producing houses during the 2000s. I show this by way of exploring a range of documentation identifying the features of new public management in initiatives funded by Arts Council England. On that basis, I proceed to analyse two Arts Council England reports, *Writ Large* and *New Writing in Theatre 2003–08* (the second referred to with the shorthand *The Dunton Report*). These texts, I show, reveal new play development dramaturgy as bureaucratic. Using scholarship on bureaucracy (e.g. Graeber 2016 [2015]), I move toward a conclusion that thickens this understanding; that, rather, it is impossible for any theatricality, and anything else, to exist outside a realm of bureaucratisation. Or, in banner dérive, we think art (and life) is bureaucracy.

In the twentieth century, new public management was a means to increase the privatisation and marketisation of public-sector institutions via enhanced managerialism. From the 1980s, there was a large-scale human resource expansion across the English education, healthcare, heritage and arts sectors. Peter Dorey (2015) writes that this process included 'the parallel imposition of a 'managerialist' regime in Britain's public services [and] the increased role of audits, inspections and other monitoring exercises to measure the performance of public services and their staff' (33). Labour deployed new public management in the arts in ways the Tories had not been able to. Cécile Doustaly and Clive Gray (2010) find, for instance, that 'the Labour governments post-1997 have effectively been more managerially interventionist into the arts sector than the Conservatives' (322). The long-established tradition of 'arms-length funding', and the detachment of arts institutions from the centre, meant the Tories had struggled to introduce new public management practices into diverse and remote arts organisations. For the Thatcher government, there was no real confidence in the arts' value. For example, Arts Council England's (1998b) report *International Data on Public Spending in the Arts in Eleven Countries* shows that public funding in the UK in the early 1990s was 0.14% of gross domestic product, much less than the arts spending from comparable countries (5). It seems that New Labour, however, saw economic and social value in the arts. As a result, they placed greater emphasis on implementing new public management.

Labour increased investment in the arts. According to Tomlin (2014), 'not only did New Labour, towards the end of its first term, virtually double the grant-in-aid available for arts funding, but there was a sense that this government understood culture to be central to the country's status and prosperity' (2). Tomlin captures the spirit of the moment here, when, initially, Labour's investment in the arts seemed to be well received. In 2002, the Treasury's *Comprehensive Spending Review* promised an annual increase in real terms of 3.5% to the arts for three years. Overall, between 1997 and 2010, not only were Arts Council England resources increased, but a further £3 billion of lottery funds was distributed to the arts (Hesmondhalgh et al. 2014: 5).

And, yet, as a pay-off for the increased funding, in order to ensure that arts organisations were demonstrating these values, Arts Council England introduced an intensified use of audit and new public management techniques (Hesmondhalgh et al. 2014: 11). I suggest that the integration of these techniques at the drop-down level of individual arts organisations is significant in assessing the potential for increased bureaucracy in the burgeoning models of play development. For example, Arts Council England generated a centralised data management system through which standard measures could be imposed across the arts to empirically evaluate social and economic impacts (Crossick and Kaszynska 2016: 16–17). The data management system meant that Arts Council England could impose new frameworks through which the arts might be assessed; these included the 'Generic Learning Outcomes' developed in 2001 and the 'Generic Social (Cultural Value) Systems' that assessed respectively the educational and social impact of artworks. Such changes meant the significant restructuring of organisations, shifts in priorities and resources, and, crucially, a splitting of activities between making art and measuring one's metrics of making art. The metrics would also include evidence of theatres focusing on generating play development activities. For example, as noted in the introduction of this Element, in 2000, Arts Council England published two reports, *The Boyden Report* and The *National Policy for Theatre in England* (2000a, 2000c). The former argued that 'new writing was failing to attract audiences' and the latter resultantly prioritised new writing, pledging funds to support growth (Arts Council England 2009a: 5). The funds arrived via the *Theatre Review* (Arts Council England 2003a) which allocated 25 million pounds intended in part for talent development. The *Theatre Writing Strategy* (Arts Council England 2003b) included recommendations that all theatre organisations should enhance training and development, their literary departments, their focus on new writing, and their playwright support (Arts Council England 2009b: 4). The writings of David Graeber (1961–2020), an American anthropologist and anarchist activist who played a key role in the Occupy movement during this period, have been influential to my understanding of English theatre's literary organisation. The aforementioned changes, for example, can be understood as part of what Graeber (2016 [2015]) refers to as an era of 'total bureaucratization' in *The Utopia of Rules* (18). Herein, Graeber studies late twentieth- and early twenty-first-century Western bureaucracy. His argument follows sociologist Robert K. Merton's (1957) definition of dysfunctional bureaucracy as 'an end-in-itself; [where] there occurs the familiar process of displacement of goals whereby an instrumental value becomes a terminal value' (11). For Graeber (2016 [2015]), bureaucracy has become entirely dysfunctional: not a means to production, but, rather an end in itself with pure deadening effects. Graeber acknowledges that in the nineteenth century, 'bureaucracy was seen as necessary for managing the market, managing democracy and also managing the modern corporation' (10–11). Over the course of the twentieth century, however, bureaucracy became a dramatically visible part of the everyday. In the 2000s, Graeber argues, there was a move towards the aforementioned total 'bureaucratization' of Western life (18). This is described as follows:

> Bureaucratic techniques (performance reviews, focus groups, time allocation surveys ...) developed in financial and corporate circles came to invade the rest of society – education, science, government – and eventually, to pervade almost every aspect of everyday life. One can best trace the process, perhaps, by following its language. There is a peculiar idiom that first emerged in such circles, full of bright, empty terms like vision, quality, stakeholder, leadership, excellence, innovation, strategic goals and best practices. (21)

Graeber offers a damning critique of the sociologist and economist Max Weber (1864–1920) as an apologist for bureaucracy – who provided a rational argument for bureaucracy now implicitly alluded to in any defence of organisational framework. In a chapter entitled 'Bureaucracy' in *Economy and Society* (956–1006), Weber (1978 [1968]) outlined six characteristics of 'Modern Bureaucracy'. These rules are rational and growth orientated, useful to any business, private or public sector, and any office great or small. They may form a particularly helpful measure, then, of the ways in which English play development practices functioned in the 2000s as a 'rational' bureaucracy that, in the way Weber envisaged, worked efficiently and productively to, as *The Dunton Report* put it, 'tackle head on issues of quality' for maximum participation in the Gross Value Added (Arts Council England 2009c: 18).

Parallel to the upscaling in new public management, in the 2000s, there was also an explosion of pioneering techniques in play development dramaturgy. These included the mass reading of unsolicited scripts, playwrights' networks, playwrights' attachments, scratch events, and one-to-one dramaturgical intervention. *Writ Large* notes an upturn in unsolicited script reading. Unsolicited script reading refers to the practice of theatres reading and perhaps commenting on scripts sent to them by playwrights, agencies, and agents. *Writ Large* argues that the 'burden of reading' at the Bush was then in the region of 1,500 scripts per year; at the 'Hampstead (1,500+), NT (1,500), Soho (2,500) and even Out of Joint (800–1,000) ... WYP (500), Liverpool Everyman and Playhouse (650), the Nuffield Theatre (250–300) ... Paines Plough (500+)' (Arts Council England 2009b: 82). The actual practice of reading scripts is documented with evidence that West Yorkshire Playhouse, for example, 'reads 300 a year, whittling them down during an intensive reading day where its readers engage in a "triage" process, reading the first ten pages of a play and then selecting those which merit a full reading and a two paragraph report' (81). The fact that theatres developed such processes is a positive shift that allowed an increased number of participants to access play development. For the first time, unsolicited scripts were receiving recognition. Theatres not only increased their dialogue with emerging playwrights via these processes, but also often used feedback as a starting point to broker new relationships with playwrights. Such mechanisms also introduced parity – for example, transparent reading of scripts limited personal taste being the barometer against which work was assessed. While offering benefits, then, to individual playwrights and to the evolution of play development approaches, the script reading processes demonstrated a number of principles recognisable from Weber's seminal account of modern bureaucracy (which I introduce in further detail later in this Element) – for instance, a system of standardisation, an adherence to rules, and the existence of a hierarchy with some scripts travelling up the levels of command. Furthermore, there is an emphasis on paperwork with the use of feedback pro formas that, as noted, significantly increase the administration in theatres and fundamentally diminish the quality and substantial commentary offered on single plays.

The Dunton Report also notes 'the emergence of online social networking sites' for playwrights as a response to writers' desires for organisations to provide 'a network between writers ... as well as fulfilling an advisory role, script library and development opportunities' (Arts Council England 2009c: 13, 17). *Writ Large* notes how 'the Bush has an ambitious new digital plan ... that will provide networking as well as feedback on new work' (Arts Council England 2009b: 73). The Bush–Green network provided an online space for playwrights to read and feedback on plays and communicate with each other about industry news. The rise in this kind of networking demonstrated another means through which play development practices were being democratised. Available as a resource to anyone via the internet, networks decentred play development resources from London and produced a range of free resources that satisfied the demand for inclusive and accessible training and peer review. Arguably, however, the networks created another bureaucratic feature. Although he observed improved communication channels, Weber could not have foreseen intranets and online forums; however, these are inevitably part of the mechanisms that Graeber references (again, as explored later in this Element). Bush–Green-type digital networks, as well as script reading services as noted earlier, can be understood as an early expression of play development as an end in itself. In other words, the service, in Merton's (1957) view, enacts a 'familiar process of displacement of goals whereby an instrumental value becomes a terminal value' (11). With playwrights' networks such as this, the instrumental value of *being in development* may supersede the terminal value of getting a production. It is my opinion that an increase in development opportunities such as these, by way of their bureaucratic functions, shifted the very meaning of play development from an activity predicated on production to an activity predicated on interminable engagement, towards 'writer' rather than 'play' development.

Another feature of new play development dramaturgy in English theatres in the 2000s was a rise in playwriting attachment schemes. An attachment is a formalised, often unpaid connection between a theatre and playwright that signals a theatre's interest in the playwright. *Writ Large* notes that 'another notable development apparent from the interviews is the flourishing of novel ways that theatres can engage with writers other than commissioning and production. . . . At the start of the survey, being under commission or a "writer-in residence" were perhaps the two most common modes connecting writers to theatres' (Arts Council England 2009b: 83–84). In the 2000s, however, they note a proliferation of attachments: 'the model derives from the practice of the National Theatre Studio where the writer is offered a two-month relationship with the theatre with no pressure to deliver a play' (84). Theatres including 'Hampstead have also started offering attachments' (73). Such attachments are extremely valuable to the individual playwright. As playwrights note, attachments engender, in some cases, a 'frustration of constantly being "in development"' (15). In this sense, we might regard attachments as potentially beneficial to individual playwrights, but structurally bureaucratic: an interminable, rather than terminal process focused on production.

In addition to networks and attachments, 'scratch events' comprised another expression of play development dramaturgy in English theatres in the 2000s. Scratch events, 'start nights', or 'rough cuts', as they are titled by Hampstead and the Royal Court respectively, comprise public showcasings of new playwriting. *The Dunton Report* notes that Contact Theatre's 'Pitch Parties' and 'Flip the Script Nights' are good examples (Arts Council England 2009c: 84). *Writ Large* offers an ambivalent reading, however: 'while most theatres now consider "rehearsed readings" not tied to productions as a misuse of resources, "rough cuts" bring in the public and offer the writer some of the dividends of having work fully staged' (Arts Council England 2009b: 86). Note that a rehearsed reading and a scratch event are only differentiated by the fact the former is 'misuse of resources' since the latter is income generating. Scratch events, *Writ Large* tells us, are another 'emphasis on this interim stage between writing and a full production' (Arts Council England 2009b: 87). Therefore, like script reading, networking sites and attachment programmes, they provided access to industry for a wide range of would-be playwrights. They can, however, be read as mechanisms that emphasise the instrumental value of development, rather than the terminal value of production. That is to say that scratch events may be rewarding to the individual playwright; however, structurally, they shift play development further away from production and closer to bureaucracy.

Finally, let us look at what *The Dunton Report* calls 'the arrival of the dramaturg [and] a more interventionist notion' of one-to-one script feedback with playwrights (Arts Council England 2009c: 80). Trencsényi (2015) defines this approach as 'professionals engaged in a dynamic dialogue-relationship with a theatre-maker . . . that is characterised by a high level of communication' (xxi). Trencsényi's definition is vague as to what the communication actually encompasses. Luckhurst (2006), however, notes that this dramaturgy relates to 'the internal structures of a play text and is concerned with the arrangement of formal elements by the playwright – plot, construction of narrative, character, time-frame and stage action' (10). According to MacDonald (2010), 'the etymology of dramaturgy suggests work, or composition, in relation to action' (93). The professionalisation of dramaturgy and the role of the dramaturg constituted a significant turn in British playmaking; playwrights, literary managers, directors, and artistic directors benefitted from the theatrical support of the new role, the democratisation of the playwright's traditional knowledge base, remit, and, finally, the greater transparency lent through enhanced collaboration.

In *Writ Large* and *The Dunton Report*, we can see the exact approaches that correspond to the dramaturgical development of the literary manager's remit. In a context which, I have argued, reinforced the need to rewrite organisational policy and administrative practices, *Writ Large* notes that during 2003–9 there occurred in building-based theatres significant 'shifts in new writing policy', the growth in 'the role of the unsolicited script', 'the growth of attachments', and 'other modes of development' including treatments and category commissions, multi-authored shows, courses, 'lock-ins', scratch events, rehearsed readings, writers' labs, and studios (Arts Council England 2009b: 71, 81, 82, 86). Where *Writ Large* focused on identifying the new pedagogical dramaturgies of literary management in building-based theatres, *The Dunton Report* evidenced emergent production-focused play development dramaturgies in companies including Graeae, Paines Plough, Contact Theatre, and Pentabus Theatre (Arts Council

England 2009c: 32–35). The report also examines new dramaturgies at fringe theatres including Theatre 503, the Ovalhouse, and the Bush Theatre (Arts Council England 2009c: 38–39). It notes an expansion of production-orientated channels including new fringe producers such as Hightide (14, 36). It also notes the emergence of pedagogical play development dramaturgies including the establishment of new writing networks such as the Bush's online forum 'Bush Green', writers' development agencies, new dramaturgy, and forms of critical intervention in a range of theatres and companies (15, 16, 16, 21).

Thus, the once-small office of literary management expanded into a new play development dramaturgy with enhanced institutional significance within individual theatres and companies. *The Dunton Report* noted that 'over the last six years there has been a perceived increase in the role of the dramaturg' (Arts Council England 2009c: 17). And, although they rarely use the word 'bureaucracy', *Writ Large* and *The Dunton Report* – as well as the aforementioned volumes by Luckhurst, Bolton, Turner and Behrndt, and Trencsényi – connect the dramaturg to a set of administrative activities suddenly underpinning new writing. These administrative activities are seen to have both positive and negative effects on production. *The Dunton Report*, for example, presents play development dramaturgy as an infrastructure intervening in new writing. At first, the report presents play development dramaturgy in positive terms, then it locates more dysfunctional aspects. Of the eighty-nine organisations and 'key individuals' surveyed, 'it was almost unanimously agreed that there has been an increase in ... development opportunities': 'most [interviewees] we spoke to were very positive ... there was a sense that the investment in development programmes has had a positive effect' (Arts Council England 2009c: 13, 14). And yet a different reading emerges: writers report a 'frustration of constantly being "in development"' and a fear that 'dramaturgy could be used as an excuse to not commit to production' (15, 18). The report warns that 'the investment in development of writers ... shouldn't be at the expense of getting productions on stage' (14). It reports playwrights describing script intervention as 'unnecessary and obstructive' with 'all sorts of things that aren't particularly helpful' (17). It concludes that 'critical interventions in new writing are of ... uneven quality' and suggests that 'the development of the role of the dramaturg [requires] further investment in the training and definition of the role' (31, 18). These readings reinforce the value of more recent works on literary management (e.g. Healy 2022), and practice in literary management itself such as those at the Bush Theatre, discussed in the conclusion of this Element.

It is *Writ Large* that presents the most ambiguous portrayal of new play development dramaturgy, celebrating its proliferation as an indicator of the health of new writing while awkwardly acknowledging its more dysfunctional aspects as an administration. For example, it repeatedly reinforces the idea that increased play development supports production: 'in general the direction of change is to provide more opportunities for successful production' (Arts Council England 2009b: 71–72). *Writ Large* provides evidence to substantiate this: 'statistical research suggests ... that the growth in development work and an increase in commissioning have happened simultaneously' (120). At the same time, the report notes that the growth in play development dramaturgies has been achieved via 'lower commitment' engagements (e.g. script reading, attachments, seed commissions, scratch nights, pitch parties, etc.) that do not necessarily result in production (84). In fact, the report defends these activities arguing that 'all the companies interviewed concur that writer development is best achieved through experience of production, but inevitably this can't always be squared with production slots' (76). In relation to the new emphasis on script feedback, the report notes the new 'burden of reading' (82). The administrative load is seen as one to require further resourcing: 'we recommend that theatres receive targeted help from the Sustain Fund to preserve their literary departments and dramaturgical activity' (125). The report also notes, however, that playwrights may not value the increased script support that *Writ Large* paradoxically calls for:

> A writer noted in the margin of his questionnaire, 'How many dramaturgs does it take to change a light bulb?', and answered 'Does it have to be a light bulb?' He captures the equivocal response we discovered to what seems to be a trend towards increasing intervention in the script. (Arts Council England 2009b: 98)

One might wonder why *Writ Large* does not pursue further interrogation of some of the negative aspects of play development dramaturgy it finds in its consultancy. I suggest this is because, as noted, new public management and its bureaucratising effects (and even its critique) had been naturalised to the extent that any problematising of its inception may have been overlooked. Luckhurst (2006), however, describes new play development as a process in which 'a new tier of functionaries embed[ed] themselves in institutions and theatre making processes' – a statement that suggests middle management inspired over-resourcing, focused on the instrumental value of play development rather than the terminal value of play production (205). Like *Writ Large* and *The Dunton Report*, Luckhurst has collected evidence from playwrights; quoting Steve Waters, for example, Luckhurst notes that play development dramaturgy is seen to be part of 'a burgeoning culture of development and a shrinking culture of production' (213) and writes that:

> [Waters and Kustow], like others, perceive the rise of literary managers and dramaturgs as little other than an unstoppable tide of Blairite bureaucrats who implement a particular New Labour pedagogy, driven by a missionary zeal for what they believe is the moral and political enlightenment of their theatre audiences. ... [Waters] regards the proliferation of literary managers as a Blairite attempt to extend the influence of a political decision-making machine that creates more layers of arbitration and prescription under the guise of democratisation. (213–214)

The weakness of analyses that assess the bureaucratic impact of play development in negative terms – that is, to what extent do literary managers and dramaturgs bureaucratise a project? – is to assume that there exists a starting point beyond the realm of 'total bureaucratization'. In the final part of this section, I signal a shift in my argument. In the preceding section, I hoped to show how evolutions in new play development were related to parallel shifts in the bureaucratic management of the arts, often observed by scholars. Now, I want to propose, instead, a bureaucracy analysis in which I employ Weber and Graeber's ideas. Here I show how play development is bureaucratic on Weber and Graeber's terms. Moreover, I argue that it is also reductive to argue whether or not play development is bureaucratic; rather, I hope to show that the whole process of making a play, from a playmaker's idea to a company's evaluation report, from the 2000s, necessarily existed within a set of rules shaped by 'total bureaucratization'.

From this perspective, an understanding of new play development in the 2000s might begin – apparently paradoxically – by noting the increasing emphasis on post-production audience experience evaluations. So quickly did the demand for evaluative data grow in response to the expectations of New Labour's agenda that, in 2005, the Independent Theatre Council, the Society of London Theatre, and the Theatrical Management Association commissioned the New Economics Foundation (NEF) to conduct 'research and create a tool usable across the whole industry to measure the impact of theatre on people's well-being' (NEF 2008: 4). As the report states, 'the theatre sector has witnessed a rising demand for evaluation and assessment of its work, and sometimes in terms of outcomes and impacts that are not directly artistic' or, as one anonymous theatre professional told researchers, 'you can make new, exciting work, but you have to dress it up as focusing on some social objective or other' (8).

The sixty-one-page report proposes feedback templates and advises on quantitative and qualitative data collection and analysis. It aims to improve the quality of data available in evaluating theatre, noting that some evaluations emphasise 'the measurement of factors that are (at least relatively) easy to quantify' and that 'this kind of evaluation puts pressure on theatre companies to produce work that scores well on these factors – that "ticks the right boxes"' (9). The report is itself an impressive bureaucratic enterprise that necessitated feedback from 'participants in our workshop at the 2007 ITC Annual Conference, the circa 2500 people who responded to our online survey and the audience members around the country who helped with our piloting by filling in a little form' (47). Why this endeavour might – paradoxically – be referenced as a starting point for play development is that it is a mainstay of feedback culture that 'a successful evaluation ... reflects on what went well and what could have been done differently, and *draws lessons for the future*' (40 (my emphasis)).

Indeed, it is not hard to find examples from the 2000s that confirm how being 'future oriented' had become a necessary part of the bureaucracy of evaluation in all sorts of theatrical endeavours; for instance, in 2007, Firebird Theatre – a company 'made up of 16 disabled actors, supported by two highly committed workers' – produced a fifty-one-page evaluation of their tour of an interpretation of Marlowe's *Dr Faustus*, which referenced, in addition to numerous types of feedback forms, 'a SWOT analysis to guide future work'; a likely condition for that future work, and the concluding point in the opportunities section of the SWOT analysis, is 'making a "business case" to ACESW for further investment' (Firebird Theatre 2007: 2, 20). For building-based theatres, then, and for touring companies alike, whatever the next thing might be, it must necessarily exist already in a context defined in part by the realm of 'total bureaucratization'.

The production and management of this bureaucratic knowledge and the demand for continuity in evaluation and planning have necessitated new specialist roles within theatres. Both *Writ Large* and *The Dunton Report* identify 'with clarity the expansion of those working with new writing in our theatre companies' (Arts Council England 2009b: 80). *The Dunton Report*, for example, notes 'the creation of new posts specialising in literary management/new writing particularly in regional venues' (Arts Council England 2009c: 26; see also 24). For example, the report notes that at theatre company Graeae, 'in 2006, a review of staffing structure led to the creation of a new role of Literary Manager' (32). Similarly, *Writ Large* notes that all twelve theatres interviewed had a literary office and manager. Furthermore, there was also evidence of a literary office hierarchy: 'a combination of a permanent member of staff overseeing a larger team' (Arts Council England 2009b: 80). For example, at the Royal Shakespeare Company, there are 'two members of staff, the Production Dramaturg (Jeanie O'Hare) and Literary Manager (Pippa Ellis [now Hill]), but also the Literary Associate (currently Anthony Neilson) and at least one of the Artistic Associates (Roxana Silbert) with a brief for new writing' (80). For a bureaucracy analysis, however, the shifts in personnel reflect an increasing engagement with the terms of a Weberian bureaucracy, including the idea that literary management possesses an office and office hierarchy. There are increasingly clearly defined job roles, a designation of authority and hiring based on skill. For example, by creating literary management hierarchies, personnel can demonstrate 'special technical expertise' (Weber 1978 [1968]: 958) in literary management – and this includes an understanding of and the ability to engage with the context of 'total bureaucratization'.

Although I have argued that bureaucracy negatively effects play development dramaturgy by shifting it towards an interminable rather than terminal process, I also have shown that the increase in play development dramaturgy has had, apparently paradoxically, enormous benefits for playwrights, playmakers more broadly, and theatres in general. The aforementioned increase in play development pedagogies had the profound effect of democratising and decentring play development, opening it out to new participants. The rise in dramaturgical practices further ensured collaboration was central to playmaking thus challenging paradigms of isolationist writerly development. Furthermore, it would be a mistake to assume that in deploying their skills these theatre professionals acted negatively on new writing – for instance, as interfering censors – rather, the deployment of their skills is what makes the production of new writing possible *within the terms of 'total bureaucratization'*. It is my opinion that the effects can be, at times, strikingly positive. Perhaps, overall, the most significant positive outcome to emerge from the increase in all play development discussed herein was its effect on inclusive commissioning. For instance, in a contribution to Roger Baines, Cristina Marinetti, and Manuele Perteghella's (2011) *Staging and Performing Translation: Text and Theatre Practice* entitled 'Not Lost in Translation', Jack Bradley outlines his contributions as the National Theatre's literary manager. In a crucial turn in English dramaturgy, Bradley notes:

> as it happened, via the NT Studio, I had routinely been working with emerging [B]lack British writers such as Tanika Gupta, Roy Williams, Ashmeed Sohoye and so on whose work then went to be produced elsewhere.... We upped the ante and invested more. The outcome: main house productions for Roy Williams, Tanika Gupta, Kwame Kwei-Armah.... When I left we were averaging almost two shows a year from writers of the [B]lack and other minority communities.... The assumption now is that the programme must include work from under-represented communities. That was a slightly left field example of gently imposing a programming strategy designed to impact on the diversity of the output. (196)

Here, Bradley signals a shift towards 'gently imposing' metrics into play development. The outcome of such a 'strategy' is, in this case, a positive one 'designed to impact on the diversity of the output'. It is important to note, however, that this positive shift also brings play development dramaturgy closer to the Graeberian definition of total bureaucracy (and thus neoliberalism) since it re-centres the activity as one deploying metrics, bureaucratic vocabularies, and continuous assessment. The problem is that innovative strategies such as Bradley's do not only exist in the applied knowledge of specialists; rather, they come to be inscribed as institutional policy. As noted, the first principle of Weberian bureaucracy is administrative rules. A new writing policy is a set of rules around a theatre's engagement with new writing, and it is through establishing and formalising such rules that play development enters a theatre's operation as a means of policing playwriting. Once the infrastructure is in place it is less receptive to the individual play and thus less effective in dynamically supporting the development of new playmaking. At the Bush (the theatre I return to in the conclusion), there was simply a desire for increasing the capacity of the theatre to identify, advocate for, and ultimately produce new work. The shift in new writing policy at these theatres demonstrates not only the increase in Weberian bureaucracy in literary management, but also that play development dramaturgy is a product of an era of neoliberal bureaucratisation.

2 Dramaturgy Factories in Key English Theatres in the 2010s

This section assesses the ways in which neoliberalism's emphasis on the transformation and restructuring of modes of production according to Fordist and post-Fordist logics was undertaken in English play development. I do this by analysing a series of interviews with practitioners of play development I conducted between 2014 and 2018. Before turning directly to that period, however, I want to start where Section 1 left off: in 2009, when the UK-based newspaper *The Guardian* published an article entitled 'The Drama Factory: How Theatre Scripts Reach the Stage' (Dickson 2009). It commenced with the rhetorical question: 'what's Britain's biggest growth industry? Playwriting, apparently'. Going on to note the literary management practices of theatres in triaging new writing, the article's aligning literary management to mass-mechanised industrial modes of production and the growth model is a critical point of debate here. The conflation of dramaturgy and manufacturing – especially at the Royal Court – conveys a certain disregard for the wider material conditions in the UK during this period. The 2008/9 recession hit manufacturing to the extent that output fell by 13% in real terms, compared to a 6% fall for the whole economy, and, in 2020, the manufacturing sector still had not recovered to its pre-crisis levels, continuing on its downward spiral that resulted in the loss of 3 million or 53% of jobs since 1981 (Rhodes 2020: 5).

Dickson's aligning of literary management with factory work is interesting in light of Section 1's claims regarding bureacratisation and standardisation, in the context of austerity as it directly impacted theatre institutions. A little later than Dickson's article, in the mid 2010s, I interviewed a group of literary managers and associates, dramaturgs, and directors with play development responsibilities about how play development worked in their buildings. As noted in the introduction of this Element, according to Arts Council England's (2009b) *Writ Large,* the most statistically significant English producers of new writing between 2003 and 2008 were West Yorkshire Playhouse (now Leeds Playhouse) (5.6%), Plymouth Drum (7.7%), the Birmingham Repertory Theatre (8.5%), the Mercury Theatre (4.2%), the Liverpool Everyman (5.1%), the Royal Exchange Theatre (5.2%), the Royal Shakespeare Company (3.1%), the Royal Court (4.9%), and the National Theatre (5.1%). Other English theatres (51%) made up the rest of the new writing produced during this period (55). What were the ways of working on new plays in these buildings and, furthermore, did they conform to wider paradigms of industrial production?

None of the practitioners of play development I interviewed, unsurprisingly, were in the habit of defining their work in Fordist or post-Fordist terms. And yet, in open-ended interviews, I observed how play development was repeatedly described as having two shared structures. I noticed continuous allusion to a first structure: a 'standard process', used at each theatre, in which the development of single-authored plays existed in dialogue with a predetermined model that understood playmaking as a journey of improvement from commissioning to production via showcasing and refinement. The 'standard process' was not quite a rigid homogenous template; its application had some flexibility and varied between theatres. A second method, which I have called the 'bespoke process', was predominantly used with commissioned artists and companies who were not working towards new writing but rather were producing new work: in this case, devised, spoken word, or alternative forms of performance. Taking the cue from those enacting English play development in the 2010s, this section materially analyses their rhetorical framing of these accounts. While creative labour is often discussed as distinct from broader conceptualisations of production (e.g. Boyle 2017), what was the relationship between English play development in the 2000s and the 'Fordist' and 'post-Fordist' capitalist modes of production during the Conservative–Liberal Democrat coalition period

(2010–15)? This transition in the economy more broadly is usually identified as reaching its peak in the 1980s, but in what follows I make a case for its relevance in the austerity period in English key new writing theatres. I rehearse both growth models and introduce their relevancy to English austerity economics – before analysing both the standard model of play development and the bespoke method against these principles. Let us return first to an understanding of Fordism.

It was Antonio Gramsci (1999 [1926]) who first theorised the burgeoning twentieth-century Fordism; his *Prison Notebooks* (558–620) advances on chapter 15 of Marx's (1990 [1867]) *Capital Volume One* entitled 'Machinery and Large-Scale Industry' (492–639). Here, Marx focuses on industrial shifts at the beginning of the second Industrial Revolution in England (which itself ran between 1870 and 1914), when small-scale capitalism was becoming increasingly complex and global, employing machinery and new technologies requiring larger factories and unions. Gramsci expands Marx's initial study. According to Robert J. Antonio and Alessandro Bonanno (2000), Gramsci

> held that the Fordist labor process ... simplified necessary operations, eliminated others, and radically routinized, deskilled and intensified labor. Accordingly, managers and technicians did all the thought work and instated comprehensive top-down control, which required operatives to work faster, more continuously, more mechanically, and in more coordinated fashion. (34–35)

Gramsci (1999 [1926]) not only documented the characteristics of Fordist manufacturing; his core concept of 'hegemony' also exposed the impact of Fordism on subjectivity: that it was a process that 'adapt[s] customs to the necessities of work' (596). Fordism is not an historic and specifically American mode of production; rather, it became increasingly integral to contemporary global manufacturing. Wayne Lewchuk (1989) provides an account of the importing of American Fordism into British industries in the early twentieth century. More recently, Abigail Hunter (2016) argues that Fordism remains central to British modes of production – for instance, in its American-imported fast food industry. Moreover, there is an established line of study that contends that the fast food industry's Fordist processes inspired other British industries that value Fordism's characteristic efficiency, productivity, calculability, predictability, and youthful workforce turnover. This has been termed the 'McDonaldization of Society' (Ritzer 1996). For Hunter (2016), McDonaldization 'draw[s] on Weber's concept of rationalisation, suggesting that society is becoming increasingly dominated by principles utilised in the fast food industry' (43). Did the production of new writing in key English theatres in the twenty-first century share any of the characteristics of Fordism or the subsequent mode of capital's production? Next is a reminder of the conditions of post-Fordism.

Post-Fordism refers to a reorganisation of capital that occurred as a response to a perceived crisis in its ability to continue to accumulate. It signals a departure from the assembly line, and also the dissolution of Fordist consumption practices including the security of ensuring one's social reproduction through work. Hall's article 'Brave New World' (1988) identified a general shift in global modes of production away from Fordism's 'classic large-scale labour processes, division of labour and class conflicts' towards this post-industrialised form of production. The global economy, Hall contends, 'has just arrived at the point where it can guarantee worldwide the standardisation of the size, shape and composition of every hamburger and every potato chip in a McDonald's Big Mac from Tokyo to Harare'. And yet these Fordist paradigms are now superseded by 'greater work flexibility [and] the maximalisation of individual choices through personal consumption' (24). Furthermore, Hall argues that 'most commentators would agree that [post-Fordism] covers at least some of the characteristics' including 'more flexible, decentralised forms of labour process and work organisation [and] a greater emphasis on choice and product differentiation' (24). In addition to pointing out the features of post-Fordist production, including rapid and powerful processing of information, the speed of knowledge production, and technological innovation, Michael Rustin (1989) argues that the new social relations require 'flatter hierarchies and greater lateral communication between members [which] are more functional for organizational goals than bureaucratic command models, in which all communication must pass up and down hierarchies or lines of command'. Following almost a decade of bureaucratic management, would English theatre's play development practices resonate with such shifts?

In segments entitled 'McTheatre', Dan Rebellato (2006: 99–103; 2009: 39–49) argues that the capitalist mode of production – Fordism – entered English theatre's own mode of production in the late twentieth century. In the 1980s, a new mode of theatrical production emerged for the staging of 'megamusicals' (Rebellato 2009: 40). Megamusicals such as *Cats* (New London Theatre, 1981) and *The Phantom of the Opera* (Her Majesty's Theatre, London, 1986) are staged in multiple venues globally. Because of this, they require efficiency, productivity, calculability, and predictability. Referencing the 'McDonaldization of Society' (Ritzer 1996), Rebellato (2009) concludes that McTheatre is 'the nearest theatre has come to being mass-industrialised' (40).

In the 2000s, Bolton (2012) identifies that English play development at the Royal Court has also mimicked capitalism's modes of production. The Royal Court's 'developmental processes are underpinned by particular assumptions regarding the form(s) and function(s) of plays' (219). Development is not simply the collaborative process of working on the commissioned play; rather it is a standardising process in which the play is structured according to an established pro forma. Bolton argues that this regulation is reproduced through a homogeneous form: as noted previously, 'the raft of new plays presented by the Royal Court in the mid-1990s proved indicative of characteristics that would become familiar' (217). In other words, a dramaturgical process was emerging in which plays were reproduced according to certain features. Development structures, however, are nonetheless seen to work according to economies of scale in which a high number of plays could be reproduced in a play development system. Bolton's reading of play development at the Royal Court shares a resemblance to Rebellato's understanding of McTheatre and yet there is a crucial difference: play development refutes *total* replicability since it constitutes a process predicated on producing multiple plays instead of just one in repeated cycles. As Bolton argues, the differences in plays produced at the Royal Court during this period are diminished on the basis of the principles deployed in development. To extend the logic of Bolton's argument further into the 2000s, it is important to return to the party political conditions shaping long-term growth and profitability, the management of the post-war Fordist economy, the counterposed model that emerged following, and crucially its manifestation in the 2010s.

Succeeding Labour's administration under Gordon Brown and led by Conservative Party Leader David Cameron and Liberal Democrat Leader Nick Clegg, the coalition accelerated the neoliberal regime advanced by previous British governments. Unlike Labour, however, who advanced an economic neoliberalism based on extending the state's reach (e.g. via public services including education and the arts), the coalition advanced the neoliberal project by advancing an aggressive individualism that focused on reducing the size of the state and public expenditure. According to Matt Beech (2015), for example, the coalition 'liberals were confident that – because of their commitment to a smaller state, market forces, lower taxes, entrepreneurship and less bureaucracy – their hour in British politics had come' (5). The principal means through which the coalition scaled back public services was via their devastating austerity programme: a set of service cuts justified on the basis that they would reduce the budget deficit in the global recession following the 2007–8 financial crisis. Writing about these shifts in 'The Neoliberal Revolution', Stuart Hall (2011) summarises the coalition as 'the most radical, far-reaching and irreversible social revolution since the war … it is arguably the best prepared ... and ambitious of the three regimes that, since the 1970s, have been maturing the neoliberal project' (718). The effects of the coalition's public-sector reformism are widely observed, not least in the arts. For example, Harvie (2015) notes how the coalition's programme affected English theatre: 'by substantially cutting state arts funding, and by promoting increased private philanthropic giving as the principle alternatives. These activities demonstrate this Conservative-led government's neoliberal commitment to cutting public infrastructure and bolstering private competition' (56).

The coalition's approach developed in the context of an earlier economic shift from one system of commodity production, Fordism, to another, post-Fordism. In relation to British industry, political economists credit the conservative regime under Margaret Thatcher, from 1979 to 1990, as the era in which Britain moved from a Fordist to a post-Fordist economy (e.g. Jessop 1989: 212; Amin 1996: 1). More recently, however, scholars have suggested that, against the twentieth-century global evolutionary narrative, Fordist structures have remained in place into the twenty-first century, often alongside post-Fordist regimes. Indeed, in Britain, the coalition, and in particular its austerity programme, advanced Britain's passage into a post-Fordist economy. As Patrick Bury and Sergio Catignani (2019) put it, under the coalition, 'the ideological blue-print for re-organising state services was supported by developments in industrial organisation, especially the end of the Fordist mode of production' (685). With this context in mind, I will now analyse the standard process and the bespoke process of play development as introduced in interview by those practising play development in the 2010s.

The Standard Process of Play Development

Key producing English theatres in the 2010s develop new writing in a structure that begins with commencing a working relationship with a playwright. There will be a setting out of the terms of the commission, including identifying what work the theatre would like the playwright to complete, over what period they would like it to be completed, and where. For example, according to Pippa Hill at the Royal Shakespeare Company, the standard process of development would commence with 'a meeting with the writer about what [the play] might be about'. In fact, Hill (2014) suggests that there may be more than one initial meeting: 'I would have a couple of one-to-ones with them'. This process of meeting initially with the playwright, prior to commission, was also an approach deployed at the West Yorkshire Playhouse and Liverpool Everyman. According to Hayley Greggs (2014) at the Liverpool Everyman, these initial meetings ensure that a potential commission 'fit with the ethos of our theatres and was right for our audiences now'. Jane Pawson at the Plymouth Drum also echoed this approach, confirming that playwrights are commissioned on the basis that they can provide a play that fits into an existing idea of future work at the theatre. For the Plymouth Drum Youth Theatre, for example, Pawson (2014) commented that 'we do about three productions a year. ... We work across age ranges. We do [one play] with eight to eleven year olds and [another that's intended for] primary-aged children. [The third is] a partnership project with our youth theatre'. If the playwright and theatre can agree to the various terms of the commission including setting a subject matter and remit (either in line with the theatre's ethos and/or target audience), the theatre commissions the playwright and establishes what Mark Rosenblatt (2014) refers to as 'the timeline of a play's development'. In the first instance, this involves setting a time frame and location for the playwright's work. The standard process, according to Hill (2014), takes 'up to two years'. The playwright will go away to write, but with the understanding that they will return for a subsequent series of development meetings. According to Suzanne Bell (2014) at the Royal Exchange Theatre, these meetings might take place 'on our stage, or in a rehearsal room'.

The development phase then commences with the theatre establishing a managerial role in relation to the playwright's ongoing task of writing the play. This involves isolating the playwright in order that they can complete their writing, but first creating a task-based framework in which the playwright can do this. The process of playwriting is thus broken down into drafting stages, with the playwright understanding that they will return for feedback on the completion of each draft. Bell commented that this approach was determined by the writer's understanding of what works best for them; however, Bell (2014) also identified that trust is important in determining the setting of these deadlines: 'most of the writers that we have under commission come from quite a long relationship within the company, [for example] we currently have under commission Simon Stephens [*Blindsided*, 2014]. ... [Development models] depend on the process of the writer'. Greggs also attested that the playwright's existing reputation and rapport with the theatre informs the way in which the theatre will divide up the playwright's task of writing. Referring to playwright Stephen Sharkey, for example, Greggs (2014) argued that 'we've had a really long relationship with him and we know his work really well. [He] pitched to Suzanne [Bell, then the literary manager] and because we trust his work ethic, and we trust his work would be right for our stages, we went ahead and commissioned him'.

Once the parameters of the playwright's work are set, the development then continues. The playwright's returned work undergoes an auditing process in which feedback and showcasing are used to evaluate the playwright's approach. For Tom Lyons (2015) at the National Theatre, the process is broken down as follows: '[the writers] do the first draft. And then we read that first draft [and] then that process becomes redrafting, notes, possibly readings in the studio'. Feedback for the playwright is offered, then, from creative collaborators at pre-determined points in the process. In the early stages, for instance following a first draft, feedback may be delivered in smaller meetings between the playwright, director and dramaturg. According to Rosenblatt (2014), 'there will be a director and/or dramaturg and actors giving suggestions … '. The playwright returns to their individual mode of working to redo their writing according to these suggestions. As Hill (2014) says, 'what often happens after that first workshop is that the writer would go and feed in all that [new] information [into] a second draft'. The next stage is for the playwright to reveal the effects of this editing, showing a revised draft to the theatre, often to a larger audience of collaborators. According to Hill, this 'often entails a group of actors, the director and me in the room'.

Chris Campbell at the Royal Court defined the feedback process in the same terms, describing how, in this second phase of development, actors enter the process to test out the playwright's work. Campbell (2014) notes that there will often be 'a reading at the end [leading to a redrafting]'. This reading of the playwright's work usually involves an extended engagement with the theatre. According to Hill (2014), this phase might comprise 'a week-long workshop'. Campbell spent some time justifying the need for these repeated interventions that lead to redrafting, suggesting that it is the theatre's opportunity to address problems inherent in the playwright's process:

> Some writers, [such as] Tim Price whose play is on now [*Teh Internet is Serious Business*, 2014] used to write a draft every week. Some people take ages and eventually produce a different play. What's interesting about drafting is there are a couple of writers who are so fertile that we try to stop them writing new drafts. Some people can turn out something that is essentially a different play. And, also, it's very interesting because I've talked to so many writers, and watched so many writers work, it's absolutely astounding to me how often they don't know what is good in their own work. I think some of them would admit it. It's partly being so close and partly the joy of creation.

Campbell suggests here the ways in which theatre staff rationalise the regulated interventions into the playwright's process: the play developers provide something lacking in the playwright's ability to assess their own writing. The showcasing and feedback is seen as remedial not only for the playwright, but also for the play. For Tony Casement at the Mercury Theatre, for example, the feedback and showcasing becomes a valve in which the formal qualities of the play might be enhanced in ways suggested by the theatre. For Casement (2014), these qualities include imbibing the play with 'things for actors to get their teeth into, that have strong emotional content, authentic relationships [and are] theatrically dynamic'. For Hill (2014), this approach has a similar remit 'giv-[ing] the writer fuel – for characterisation . . ., but to also ask questions about the shape of the play and where we are with it'.

The final stage in the development is to audit the extent to which the playwright has met the terms of their commission by introducing other theatrical systems as a means for evaluation and progression. If these experiments in integrating systems, including movement, sound, lighting, and design, do not yet suggest an internal coherence on terms determined by the theatre, the playwright will return to their task and make changes to their work. Hill (2014) describes this approach as follows: 'We commissioned Ella Hickson to write [*Wendy and Peter Pan*, 2013]. We had two workshops where we were really looking to see how the script was working. And then we had one mixed workshop – script and stage craft. We needed to find a theatrical language. That's a kind of rough outline of a model'. As a footnote, Hill also argued that previews offer the theatre a final opportunity to assess and make changes to a new theatrical work in performance. How do these descriptions of the standard process of play development in key new writing theatres thus conform to the Fordist or post-Fordist mode of production?

The standard process reflects characteristics of standardisation – the most obvious characteristic of Fordist production; the play passes along a production line, assessed en route through a series of small tasks for which individual workers are responsible. This process is represented as one that, as Bell (2014) says, 'depend[s] on the process of the writer' – what works best for them and their existing modes of creativity. Such a comment reveals a positive evolution in the organisation of play development observed in Section 1 in operation in the preceding decade. It enhances, for example, levels of planning and rationalises production. Its systematisation is intended to support the productivity of the playwright who returns work at regular intervals thus enhancing the efficiency and success of the theatre's commissioning and programming models. Moreover, the process enhances planning and resource efficiency for production, allowing theatres to plan for human and material costs by seeing the work and its requirements develop incrementally. The evaluation process in development can also limit economic risk in playmaking since suggestions can be made on a cost basis; for example, if a playwright has written excessive characters or design features into their play, these can be omitted or reduced. The standard process of development, then, particularly the feedback and showcasing stages, allows these theatres to introduce what Hunter argues are the benefits of Fordism in contemporary production: efficiency, productivity, calculability, and predictability. Paradoxically, however, the standardisation also prioritises the autonomous, flexible, and self-organised work of the playwright – key attributes of post-Fordist working. This demonstrates that the standard model might appear Fordist, but may actually be rooted in a more recent post-Fordist culture of intellectual, creative, and immaterial labour. During the mid 2010s, theatres' use of the standard process of play development was seen as entrenched in as well as shifting towards a new model. Love (2015) identifies that 'collaborative ways of working are gaining momentum at the same time as a certain structure of playwriting – with a notion of the author firmly at its centre – is reinforced' (122). The more recent bespoke process of play development at these theatres is key to evidencing the shifting economic rationality of theatre's modes of production towards that of post-Fordism.

The Bespoke Process of Play Development

In relation to the development of new work, I observed how a bespoke mode of development was now applied at theatres. At the West Yorkshire Playhouse, for example, Rosenblatt (2014) described the bespoke approach that was being undertaken with the company RashDash:

> Now we're embracing a much more collaborative process. ... And there is determination to explode that [standard process]. One of our associate companies called RashDash are two theatre makers who dance, and sing, and write text. [They're working with a] writer who we have on attachment here, Alice Birch, to create a piece [*We want you to watch*, 2015]. Their process is much more complicated [and] time consuming. It's a group of people working out [questions such as] "who is doing this?", "whose idea is leading this?" ... And a lot of this is to do with the fact that text is not always at the centre of the process. It's text and movement and form. ... So that's a very different model, but equally that has lots of R&D support and we provide that.

The bespoke process is presented here by Rosenblatt as a self-organised, non-hierarchical working arrangement between theatrical collaborators determined by the artists themselves. The playwright, inside the bespoke process, in this case Alice Birch, is seen working alongside RashDash, developing the play text not as an individual unit, but as a thread sewn into the other theatrical systems that RashDash are building simultaneously. The question 'whose idea is leading this?' is, then, important; there seems to be an acknowledgement that, in the bespoke process, traditional ideas of the play and playwright and the assumed power structures surrounding them are herein reappraised. As Rosenblatt (2014) says: 'text is not always at the centre of the process' and there is a 'determination to explode' preceding conventions. Neither the playwright, nor their play, nor the standard process of development, then, is leading this particular approach. For example, Rosenblatt's presenting this model as a decentring of power suggests that the standardised play development markers surrounding the playwright, including the processes of redrafting and gradual inclusion of individuated theatrical units, are omitted. Instead, the first feature of the bespoke model of development seems to be a non-hierarchical, collaborative approach that equalises contributors. Furthermore, the bespoke process is seemingly synchronous rather than linear; theatrical systems are co-developed rather than introduced following the isolated completion of the script.

The presentation of the bespoke process as a non-hierarchical arrangement also extends to the theatre's role. Rosenblatt's account, for example, seems to suggest that oversight from the West Yorkshire playhouse is omitted from at least some of the development activity since their contributions are not emphasised. Instead, what is presented is an account in which the conventional social relations between the theatre and artists, including quality-assurance mechanisms, are reduced. There seems to be the presentation of a decentralised, informal, non-managed, and non-regulated playmaking in which the commissioned artists work collaboratively but independently to develop the work. The implication, then, is that power structures and managerial forces are absented from the bespoke process; however, Rosenblatt clearly has strong knowledge and oversight of the development. Rosenblatt's own understanding of the process suggests that the theatre's governance is not necessarily absent here; rather, social relations are represented in a way that plays down conventional play development power structures. The bespoke process is, then, presented as informal, egalitarian, and hierarchy-free on all fronts, though, as we have seen, these qualities are not a departure from capital's mode of production, but characteristics of a post-Fordist evolution. As Hall (1988) argued, post-Fordist modes of production operate via 'more flexible, decentralised forms of labour process and work organisation' (24). Here, the decentralising of theatrical social relations in development is seen as paramount to the bespoke process.

The bespoke process, unlike the Fordist standard model, does not maximise efficiency via the production line's time and motion principles. Instead, Rosenblatt (2014) contends, the bespoke process is 'more complicated [and] time consuming'. Here, then, the artists seem to determine their own timekeeping as a new means for maximising efficiency. This evolution is characteristic of a post-Fordist negotiation of working time, as we have observed, in which the capitalist mode of production has shifted from a demarcated working day to a more fluid arrangement that, as Mylonas (2011) observes, 'relies on a rationality of flexibility that blends work with free time' (2). The temporal arrangements of the bespoke process engender a further post-Fordist quality to this play development structure. They contribute to a more project-focused approach – itself another post-Fordist working principle according to Zygmunt Bauman (2005). The notion of the project reinforces, I suggest, the rejection of conventional work scheduling and deadlines. Rosenblatt emphasises the project-based approach, again, as a series of questions (e.g. 'who's doing this?'). These questions are not easily answered and therefore suggest an endurance and interminability to the project framework as well as a focus on immaterial, abstract, and conceptual labour. For example, the abstract and philosophical qualities to the questions require both persistent and repeated attention, suggesting a protracted need for examination. Moreover, they are also cerebral and thus portable – for example, even when the artists aren't 'working', they will be able to take these questions with them and reflect on how they might be addressed. The bespoke process thus deploys 'continuous development': a durational approach that resists the conventional demarcated, material, task-based, and timekeeping model of standard play development and instead ensures efficiency through the process of reflexively tracking formal and informal abstract aspects of play development. What we can start to see here is that bespoke play development *seems* to be free from the formal constraints of work, but, paradoxically, the labour efficiency of artists is produced in different ways – a point I return to.

The bespoke process of play development can also now be observed within the standard model currently being deployed for single-authored plays. For example, Pawson emphasised that, even with playwrights on pre-designed writing briefs for the Youth Theatre, there was now an understanding that the process should possess the qualities described by Rosenblatt: the play development should be flexible, non-hierarchical, time-fluid, project-focused, and immaterial. Pawson (2014) said: 'we want it to develop organically from what they're interested in. Sometimes we ask "what's the next play you want to write?" and if it's something that we might be interested in then we'll go from there. That's the emphasis. We place it on the writers.' Pawson thus reimagines the standard process here on increasingly post-Fordist terms: it is presented as artist led, without demarcated managerial quality assurance and, furthermore, determined by questions that represent theatrical labour as flexible with diffuse timekeeping arrangements and a project base. A complex social relationship is thus created in which the theatre once again plays down the managerial role (in this case, the tightly framed commissioning of the Youth Theatre's brief) and represents the playwright's labour as a set of entrepreneurial freedoms including the self-setting and organising of theatrical work.

Casement, Greggs, and Bell also presented an increasingly bespoke interpretation of the standard practice of play development. As Casement (2014) says: 'it depends what [play] it is, but broadly speaking, it's [our] imaginative response to the material'. Greggs (2014) noted that 'it depends so much on where plays come from'. Moreover, Bell noted that, when working with playwrights, there was now an emphasis on challenging how their process should be demarcated and undertaken. Bell (2014) commented that 'some writers want workshops where actors completely pull apart their script and they work very freely and improvise, and other writers just want a group of actors for half a day to read their work. ... Some writers want a workshop with a movement director or a sound designer just so that they can unlock something'. Bell's comments suggest that it is the playwrights themselves who are driving more flexibility into the standard model of development, nudging it to operate as a bespoke model of development on the terms described by Rosenblatt. By requesting workshops with other collaborators including movement and sound designers, playwrights are, as Love suggests, forcing the development structures at these theatres to operate on increasingly bespoke terms that embed further collaborative and non-hierarchical ways of working. It is perhaps Tessa Walker (2015) at the Birmingham Rep who offers the most instructive example of the bespoke development process. Walker argues that:

> There really is no one way to do it. Plays are living, breathing things and they'll ask very different things of you as a director, as an actor, as someone working with the play in development. The answer is I don't really know [how to develop a play], but I do know that they – and the people that are writing it – will need different things. ... There isn't a way to develop plays, but, there is, I suppose, an attitude with which you respond to the thing that it is for whatever it means at that moment.

I suggest that Walker advances an idea of play development as a post-Fordist mode of production and consumption. For example, as Hall (2014) noted, post-Fordism has evolved in relation to 'the maximalisation of individual choices through personal consumption' (24). Presented as a mode of production with heightened individualism awarded through flexibility, we can understand Walker's concept of play development within the post-Fordist paradigm. First, Walker presents the play as a unique artefact that 'will ask very different things of you ... as someone working in play development'. The play as a unique artefact, then, necessarily demands a post-Fordist approach to production since they 'need very different things'. Walker's statement demonstrates how compelling post-Fordist modes of production in play development sound. As was noted at the 2009 ICA 'Art and Post-Fordism conference', in the contemporary arts, an increase in casual, project-based, and highly individuated labour processes is often prized because they give the 'allure of freedom [and] flexible working hours'. The bespoke 'attitude' that Walker describes is alluring since it understands post-Fordist qualities as a commonsensical, desirable, and indeed increasingly necessary condition of playmaking. After all, the aforementioned characteristics of the bespoke model seemingly offer the artist freedom, flexibility, and a unique response to their work. Furthermore, as Bell shows us, these conditions are in line with what artists desire as composite features of commissioned play development. As with Rosenblatt, Walker makes clear that this revised 'attitude' contrasts starkly to the oppositional model of standard play development which, paradoxically, does not individuate playmaking in the way play developers and artists now see as ideal. It is important to remember, though, that it is *because* of its post-Fordist qualities that the bespoke mode of development appears to be an improvement on the standard model. In 2014–15, the bespoke process seemed to be becoming increasingly hegemonic in key new writing theatres; for example, Bell (2014) suggested that playmakers were increasingly requesting more flexible working arrangements. By explicitly stating the bespoke practice as their mode of play development, then, theatres demonstrate to artists that their models are conducive to current conceptions of play development best practice and are, more broadly, aligned with post-Fordist ideals of wage labour now. Herein, I tried to show how neoliberalism's emphasis on transformation and restructuring informed the mode of production of English play development during 2014–18. But what of the artists inside these factories?

3 'You Say You Suffer from a Gentle Schizophrenia': Artistic Subjectivity inside English Play Development in the 2010s

Azunwo Ezwho Emenkie (2014) defines playwriting as a 'scholarly activity engineered by creative imagination. It is the art and techniques of dramatic compositions and theatrical representation. Therefore it is not merely a [text] but a creative one that articulates the vision of the dramatist in a given period of human experience' (9). In this section, I expand Ezwho Emenkie's exploration by advancing an analysis of the playwright inside the social, political, and economic environment of English new writing theatres in the 2010s. I am interested in showing the extent to which artistic subjectivity was shaped, between 2014 and 2018, according to neoliberal paradigms. By using the same approach of practitioner interviews, this time with artists, I explore the self-conception of commissioned playwrights in the English structures of play development. Artistic subjectivity is that which Thet Shein Win (2014) defines as the 'idea that what [artists] produce is, in part, a reflection on themselves' (2). In particular, I ask how artistic subjectivity is structured within the context of English play development during this decade. What is a playwright's artistic identity inside a commissioning model and the creative labour market determined by the neoliberal project? For this purpose, I make a connection between theorising on artistic and neoliberal subjectivity and testimonies from playwrights commissioned in the mid 2010s at the theatres introduced earlier. I bring together commentary from playwrights and playmakers Amanda Wittington (*Saturday Night Sunday Morning*, 2014, Mercury Theatre), Oladipo Agboluaje (*Immune*, 2015, Plymouth Drum), RashDash (*We Want You to Watch*, 2015, Leeds [formerly West Yorkshire] Playhouse), Lee Mattinson (*Crocodiles*, 2014, Manchester Royal Exchange), Phil Porter (*The Christmas Truce*, 2014, Royal Shakespeare Company), Tim Price (*Teh Internet is Serious Business*, 2014, the Royal Court), Daniel Matthews (*Scrappers*, 2013, Liverpool Everyman and Playhouse), Steven Camden (*Backdown*, 2015, Birmingham Repertory Theatre), and Alexander Zeldin (*Beyond Caring*, 2014, National Theatre). By interviewing commissioned artists about their experiences of play development at these theatres in the mid 2010s, I focus on artistic subjectivity inside the aforementioned modes of production. How does artistic self-presentation map onto discourses of neoliberal subjectivity? I suggest that the commissioned artist's subjectivity inside the play development 'factory' is a complex amalgamation of artistic and neoliberal subjectivity, where artistic subjectivity is ipso facto imbricated with the neoliberal. First, an engagement with existing accounts of the interrelationship of neoliberal and artistic subjectivity: I provide an extended account of neoliberal artistic subjectivity and map it onto the austerity period in Britain. I bring together different examples of artistic subjectivity to provide a framework through which to analyse the interviews with artists following.

In the context of the coalition government (2010–15), playmakers, alongside all UK subjects, would be under pressure to conceive of themselves as units of human capital. The Cameron-Clegg Anglo-Liberal model for growth was predicated on stimulating further labour power in Britain by using the reserve army of unemployed, but also through broadening the notion of work according to post-Fordist paradigms. For example, the 'Work Programme', a nationwide initiative intended to get unemployed people back to work, was a flagship welfare-to-work scheme, instated in June 2011. It was, as Jay Wiggan (2015) puts it, 'ostensibly about securing job outcomes across a diverse body of non-employed labour power using economic rationality to drive performance' (385). The Work Programme is one example of the neoliberal economic rationality that was characteristic of coalition policy. According to Craig Berry (2014), for instance, under the coalition 'finding a job – any job – [was] prioritised above all other considerations' (606). Berry argues that, in response, citizens were compelled to develop rapidly as neoliberal subjects: 'individuals, therefore, had to be both correctly incentivised to accept available employment opportunities, and capable of adapting to potentially volatile labour market conditions once in employment' (594). An ideal expression of the neoliberal subject prominent during the coalition period was the entrepreneur – the individual capable of adapting to the volatile labour market by ensuring their own self-employment and taking on their own financial risks. According to Nima Sanandaji (2014), 'one of the most striking features of the economic recovery has been the record 4.5 million Britons who are now self-employed. Ian Duncan Smith (2014) claimed that this was evidence that the coalition was "reviving Britain's entrepreneurial spirit"'. Indeed, in 2014, The Centre for Entrepreneurs in Britain released 'The Entrepreneurial Manifesto' which celebrated the growth of entrepreneurialism in Britain.

Michel Foucault's theorising on neoliberal subjectivity is relevant to understanding such biopolitical evolution. In *The Birth of Biopolitics: Lectures at the Collège de France, 1978–1979,* Foucault contended that liberalism's laissez-faire approach to the market was shifting. The market was no longer based on exchange but, rather, increasingly predicated 'toward the multiplicity and differentiation of enterprises' (149). As Colette Conroy (2010) notes, 'Foucault suggests that the body is used as a way of placing human beings within a regulatory system' (loc. 463). Since the regulatory system was the market, Foucault (2008) argues that 'what is sought is not a society subject to the commodity ... the homo economicus sought after is not the man of exchange or man the consumer; he is the man of enterprise and production' (147, 149). What Foucault means by this is that Marx's concept of capitalist reproduction via physical labour power and its abstraction in exchange has evolved. In the twentieth century, capitalism is embodied. Wendy Brown elucidates Foucault's conception of the neoliberal subject. When exchange is replaced by competition as the dialectic of capitalist reproduction, human subjects are envisioned not as the labour power which, as Marx's value theory has it, is congealed in objects through commodity production; rather, humans become human capital by consuming their own labour power. Thus, as Brown (2015) puts it, 'productivity is prioritized over product; enterprise is prioritised over consumption' (65–66). Leigh Claire La Berge clarifies Foucault's re-conceptualisation of work and subjectivity further as 'the self-narration of a subject as one who is compelled to sell his or her labor under less than free conditions has expired. Now the subject will understand herself as possessor of "human capital" who seeks a return on her investment'. La Berge (2019) contends that Autonomist theorists, namely Negri (2017) and Hardt and Negri (2001), 'ultimately end up borrowing from Foucault' in what would become an anti-Marxist trajectory of theorising on subjectivity at the end of the twentieth century (23).

Experientially, artists in English play development evolved dramatically in the twentieth and twenty-first centuries, becoming increasingly professionalised and entrepreneurial. I suggest that the stories artists told about themselves in public forums during this period can serve as an example of this shift. For instance, I recall a workshop in the mid 2010s with an acclaimed English theatre company. The lead artists were remembering how previously they never used to bother with Arts Council grant applications. At the time, they believed themselves not to be sufficiently organised nor engaged. Instead, they chose to fund their theatre practice by personal credit card debt in advance of Edinburgh runs, hoping to make back the loss through ticket sales (unless, of course, they spent their earnings in other ways). Such transgressive tales of play development in the 1990s were, as was the case in the workshop I attended, a means through which artists paradoxically *revealed* themselves to be ideal neoliberal subjects in the twenty-first century, in line with Luc Boltanski and Eve Chiapello's (2018 [1999]: 139) reading. During this period, artists had become more adept (or were more comfortable with *saying* they were) at having separate income streams, accounting systems, 'side hustles', and grant writing expertise. They told us in subtle ways that they had become skilled at speculation, risk aversion, and proof-of-concept sharing that ameliorated the funding of poor-quality work. They became confident at talking about themselves too – for example, in workshops at theatres on their approach to 'being an artist'. Harvie (2013) is known for commenting on the historical material evolution of the artist during this period, whose characteristics made them 'artrepreneurs' (62–108).

How did artists get so good at telling people about their new business acumen? Harvie's critique can be extended to expose the origin story: the careers and employability discourses that were a key critical feature in the neoliberal transformation of higher education during this time (Giroux 2014). Here, in the mandatory modules on 'careers in the creative industries', students' burgeoning theatre knowledge became the vehicle of such self-branding. Knowledge of theatre systems including scenography, direction, and dramaturgy, for example, manifest the visual and typographical pseudo-performance of creativity that any young theatre professional's personal website might boast. It is important to note that, in becoming more entrepreneurial, however, would-be artists could also become increasingly self-sufficient and generally more 'employable' – the aim of universities and, beyond that, the UK Government. While the economic rationality at the heart of the 'artrepreneur' is therefore beyond dispute, Harvie (2013), though, presents the damaging effects of this re-conceptualisation of the artist, the art, and also its development process since this shift 'obliges art relentlessly to pursue productivity, permanent growth and profit' (62–63). Artrepreneurial positionalities become both ubiquitous and ridiculous, then, in the same moment. In Sh!t Theatre's *Dollywould* (2018), for example, the company members laugh at 'all the lies we had to tell the Arts Council!' vis-à-vis the pursuit of funding to actually go to the Dollywood Theme Park in Tennessee, USA (the subject of the performance). This may seem like a reversal to the 1990s and a rejection of the terms of artrepreneurialism. It works in the same way, however, as the story from the workshop. We laugh along because we play/don't play the game too.

In order to properly resist appropriation, artists must, as Harvie (2013) puts it, become – instead – craftspeople (97). Craftsmanship displays qualities that challenge entrepreneurialism's drive to profit. These include an emphasis on working 'with difficulties, resistance and ambiguity'; to not prioritise 'efficiency and productivity, but simply quality'; for practice to be conceived as a process 'not "as a fixed set of things"'; and, furthermore, that 'craftsmanship is egalitarian' (92, 97, 98). In signalling the need to move beyond English play development contexts, Harvie's work aligns with that of Nicholas Ridout (2013) – who 'look[s] at the theatre as a place and a practice where it might be possible to think disruptively about work and leisure, about work and love, and about the apparently separate realms of necessity and freedom' (4). Exploring (predominantly) industrial and post-industrial capitalist European and American contexts in the twentieth and twenty-first centuries, Ridout traces a subversive figure throughout theatre's history that, paradoxically, resists capital's claim on artistic subjectivity. Somewhat reminiscent of Harvie's craftsman, Ridout seeks to locate the personification of 'passionate amateurs' in theatre. The figure of the passionate amateur is found in a range of diverse contexts and established as 'the person, either knowingly or not, in pursuit of . . . resistance to the establishment of our now dominant understanding of the relations between work and time' (6). In my experience, English play development continues to enable artists to practise across unforeseen durations, sometimes extending development phases into decades. Arts Council England is also aware of the sometimes lengthy gestation phase of certain creative works – for divergent reasons.

The passionate amateur, however, Ridout claims, is a figure similar to the romantic anti-capitalist who personifies 'a resistance to industrial capitalism, articulated on behalf of values, practices, and experiences, often those of a premodern, preindustrial, rural life, that industrial capitalism seemed determined to destroy' (6). Ridout suggests not only that the passionate amateur exists in theatre's history, but that theatre in general performs what he refers to as a 'detour' in the trajectory of capital in which the time stands still and therefore the construct of time that determines neoliberalism is refused entry

(9). Will the passionate amateur, and Ridout's ideal of theatre, be found in English play development during this period?

Bojana Kunst asserts that artists such as this might be tricky to find. Kunst thematically elaborates on similar questions to Harvie and Ridout, but in relation to predominantly (Eastern) European performance, dance and choreography. *Artist at Work* explores the effects of neoliberalism on artistic subjectivity including examining the ways in which Belgian philosopher Dieter Lesage summarises the work of the artist Ina Wudtke. According to Kunst (2015), Lesage describes what Wudtke actually does when she works as an artist:

> You are an artist and that means: you don't do it for the money. That is what some people think. It is a great excuse not to pay you for all the things you do. So what happens is that you, as an artist, put money into projects that others will show in their museum, in their Kunsthalle, in their exhibition space, in their gallery. So you are an investor. You give loans nobody will repay you. You take financial risks. You speculate on yourself as an artistic asset. You are a trader. You cannot put all your money into one kind of artistic stock. So you diversify your activities. You manage the risks you take. You would say it differently. I know. You say you suffer from a gentle schizophrenia. You have multiple personalities. (134)

Kunst sets out a number of ways in which artists can be 'disobedient' to the logic of capital (178). One way is for the artist to re-conceptualise their relationship to work. Is it possible to determine our practice against the flow of post-Fordist constructs including productivity, transformation, and flexibility? Like the Sh!t Theatre example, we can view many artistic practices and ways of working as having an interesting relationship with what Kunst calls non-work: mistakes, minimum effort, coincidence, duration, passivity, etcetera. (183). Diverging from human capital's focus on entrepreneurialism, competition, and cost for benefit self-care, such terms correspond to qualities of craftsmanship noted by Harvie- in particular, the emphasis on inefficiency and slowness. More obviously, however, they are aligned with Ridout's description of passionate amateurism. This section follows these cues, complexities, and my own focus on rhetorical and performative presentations to identify the ways artists construct themselves in English play development in the 2010s.

Artistic Subjectivity in English Play Development in the 2010s

Attracting Investors and Brand Marketability

In an interview, each artist described the process of achieving their commission and entering into play development. In order to commence a facilitated play development phase in key English theatres, playmakers must attract theatrical investors and demonstrate brand marketability. Although this sample is not representative, I noticed that all artists I interviewed described a general performance of attracting investors through brand marketability. Personal branding is closely aligned with the qualities of human capital, artrepreneurialism, and artistic visibility as defined by Brown, Harvie, and Kunst respectively. It focuses on self-presentation and subtle self-commodification. In the realm of mainstream playwriting, the playwright's brand may be largely reliant on an established repertoire of economically successful performances, but also on established social relations in the professional theatre-making community. Tim Price, whose play *Teh Internet is Serious Business* was in development at the Royal Court in 2014, evidenced how possessing – and reiterating – one's brand is key to securing a commission. As a playwright with a history of stage plays and strong connections to directors, designers, literary managers, etcetera, Price (2014) said he simply 'wrote to [the Royal Court] and said that I wanted to do a play about [the] Anonymous [movement]'. The implication was a commission swiftly followed. Price's approach, I suggest, demonstrates the ways in which a playwright's brand supports their access to play development. It shows play development's connection to competitive paradigms of neoliberal subjectivity in which playwrights must compete for production slots on the basis of to what extent their brands and networks are established. In line with Harvie, I suggest there is much to be gained by playmakers in securing and maintaining a personal brand. For example, with brand power, playmakers (and their brokering agents) 'foster such business-related skills as raising, managing and diversifying resources of finance; cultivating institutional and/or personal development' (Harvie 2013: 74). For other, less-established artists, their more modest brand seemed to create more precarious terms on which they could secure production: more a case of, as Luttickken puts it, 'being in the right place at the right time' (in Lesage 2012: 16). For example, playwright Lee Mattinson secured a commission in 2014 for *Crocodiles* at the Royal Exchange Theatre by entering a competition. This involved a self-organised trajectory including completing the play without commission in advance, facilitating a read-through, and securing collaborators including director Ng Choon Ping. Similarly, for RashDash's *We Want You to Watch* (2015) at the National Theatre, their self-organised and funded engagements with different venues prior to commission culminated in a coverage process at Battersea Arts Centre. Moreover, they were requested to provide live demonstrations of their prospective brand marketability at invitation-only showcasings. These live showcasings of brand potential seem currently unevenly integrated into the commissioning of new work.

Playwrights had to similarly showcase prospective brand marketability. For example, Danny Matthews' play *Scrappers* (2013) at the Liverpool

Everyman was commissioned only after a rigorous drafting and showcasing process in the writers' group. Both playwrights and playmakers were therefore expected to undertake unpaid work prior to commission via pitching, entering competitions, and showcasing to demonstrate their own (and their projects') prospective viability. Since established playmakers have historically found production more readily accessible, we cannot necessarily claim these performances as especially neoliberal. As we continue to analyse the nuances of brand demonstration, I suggest artistic subjectivity in play development, however, becomes increasingly aligned with that of human capital. For example, activities including pitching, entering competitions, and showcasing bear structural resemblance to the compulsory performance of the human subject as Brown describes it. Brown (2015) argues that units of human capital must 'maximise their capital value in the present and enhance their future value … through practices of … self-investment and/or attracting investors' (22). Furthermore, the general performance of the artist is predicated on 'leveraging its competitive positioning and enhancing its monetary and non-monetary portfolio value' (10). Commissioning structures thus seem to ask playmakers to *become* human capital; the more human capital in evidence, the more likelihood of entering play development. New projects, it seems, are assessed by both artists and commissioning theatres, as Read (2009) puts it, 'according to a particular calculation of cost for benefit' (28). The artist seemingly will agree to perform as human capital to the extent to which a potential opportunity for commission arises from it. On the other hand, the commissioning theatre will commission work on the basis that artists demonstrate their adherence to their performance as human capital via, in the first instance, brand power. Artists do achieve a commission via a performance as human capital, supported by the theatre, but this performance is not naturalised and is replete with difficulties and uncertainties.

Although it was clear that brand power in play development was key to attracting investors, in interviews, playmakers were often at pains to emphasise that development *did not* start with the demonstration of brand marketability. Rather, play development was emphasised as having commenced with moments of coincidence: a characteristic of 'non-work' and feature of the 'doing less' performance according to Kunst (2015: 183) and of non-productive sociality according to Ridout. In an interview, for example, Greenland of RashDash (2017) discussed how their collaboration with Birch started as a coincidence:

> The [Creative Director at Transform Leeds] and West Yorkshire Playhouse said 'what do you think is the thing you could really do with to move forward with your work?' We said 'work with a writer'. We started to put together a short-list of women writers. Alice [Birch] was on that list [of feminist writers we wanted to work with]. When we met, we really got on and we had loads of similar political and radical feeling.

Even though RashDash seemed to represent the commissioning of Birch as informal, romantic (in Ridout's sense) and even non-hierarchical, this assembling of creatives, however, is not quite the same as Kunst's understanding of coincidence or indeed Ridout's description of passionate amateurism. This is because Birch's entry into the project ostensibly supported the productive labour and upskilling of RashDash by locating human capital's qualities including branding and professional development. It is the same for playwrights. Matthews also argued, for example, that his commission by the Liverpool Everyman started as a coincidence. Although *Scrappers* was Matthews' first produced play, he had studied for a degree in drama at Liverpool John Moores University, gained a place on the Everyman's prestigious writing programme, and had received numerous staged readings. As a result, it can be assumed that he had a solid understanding of theatrical practice and brand marketability on the Liverpool writing scene. Furthermore, following the production of *Scrappers*, Matthews went on to work as Creative Learning Producer at The Dukes, Lancaster, where he teaches and facilitates playwriting. Despite this, Matthews (2017) suggested during an interview that he had 'no preconceptions of what a piece of theatre should be. It was just me talking about thoughts and feelings'. Similarly, Steven Camden (2017) argued that being commissioned to make a piece of theatre was a coincidence, rather than a career plan: 'I'm not from a theatre background. I'm also not massively enamoured by a lot of the theatre that I've seen in terms of feeling myself represented, and [the issues], and people, that I grew up with. . . . It was never about 'one day I'll have a play on at the National or wherever.' By this point, Camden was one of the UK's most acclaimed spoken-word artists who had toured globally; he was a lead artist for Ministry of Stories and The Roundhouse poetry collective and, by 2013, the creative director of BearheART, a story-based creative projects company. By underplaying their brand marketability and emphasising instead coincidence, artists seem to aim to rhetorically resist the paradigms of human capital. Artists may choose to represent themselves as resisting neoliberalism's parameters, in much the same way that other groups of workers – including academics, say – do. They are, however, inevitably and unconsciously shaped by the frameworks of human capital.

Work Ethic and Flexibility

Playmakers responded rapidly, following initial meetings, to the theatres' commission briefs. For example, in all cases, playmakers committed to a development timeline and schedule. In some cases, the tasks against which playmakers had to demonstrate their work ethic were complex and, in my opinion, stretched the limits of the contract. For example, when playwright Oladipo Agboluaje (2017) was commissioned to write *Immune* (2015) for the Plymouth Drum, 'he was under the illusion that it would be 'come in, sit down, and then [go away] and write whatever you want to'. In reality, however, the commission involved developing a play for performance by three Youth Theatres simultaneously – in other words, three commissions for the price of one.

Immune thus required an expanded remit around Agboluaje's role that included delivering workshops with the three youth theatres and responding creatively to the material the young people generated. In addition, Agboluaje's process necessitated working flexibly between three locations in Plymouth, Northampton, and Leeds. Agboluaje noted that 'I wasn't solely the writer. I was also the workshop facilitator. ... It was much more daunting than I'd [anticipated].' Agboluaje's comments suggest that the expected qualities of human capital – their work ethic and flexibility – not only inform the playwright's work allocation, but also fundamentally revision the playwright's labour as solitary and self-set. Instead, as is proper for human capital, the playwright is expected to work more, demonstrating their capacity for labour in any way dreamt up by the commissioning theatre. Moreover, playwrights also described how they demonstrated work ethic by attending as closely as possible to the terms of the brief. For example, at the Royal Shakespeare Company, for *The Christmas Truce* (2014), Phil Porter (2014) noted how he was 'sent a pack. It was about Bruce Bairnsfather who was a humourist, cartoonist, and originally from Stratford. He actually worked in the theatre – he put up their original lighting. He'd written about the Christmas truce. I knew that he would be a part [of the play], but how I used him was up to me'. Although Porter emphasised the self-determined nature in which he could respond to the brief, there was also a sense that the 'pack' constituted a way in which Porter must display his qualities as a neoliberal subject, showcasing an expanded approach to work and the playwright's increasingly elastic flexibility in terms of interpreting the theatre's requests.

The approaches described by playwrights, I suggest, demonstrate an emphasis on extra work added into the process, with the commissioned writer either being suggested or suggesting further ways in which they might demonstrate the qualities of human capital. Again, the commissioned artists' performance as human capital is not naturalised; rather, it often presents as a surprise or difficulty to the artists. Nevertheless, this extra work in play development seems congruent with the coalition's emphasis on working more – and even, as Berry (2014) puts it, on 'finding a job – any job' (606). Moreover, the emphasis on additional work seems to embed Luttickken's idea of the general performance into play development; networking does not stop at the commissioning phase, but is rather carried into the project as a central working approach in which the playmaker must be tasked with workshops and additional engagements as part of the process. Human capital is thus always on duty; as Brown (2015) argues, its '*constant* and ubiquitous aim ... is to entrepreneurialize its endeavors' (36). The emphasis on demonstrable work ethic and flexibility in play development also connects with Harvie's reading of the artrepreneur who must continue to demonstrate work ethic and flexibility at all times. By modelling human capital's work ethic and flexibility in play development, however, artists may benefit substantially. They can cultivate goodwill from collaborators by working more flexibly. In addition, they can foster a range of innovations in their practice (such as working across several commissioned projects at once) in ways that generate further interest and enhance brand power and the likelihood of future work. Work ethic, then, has value in play development in terms of stimulating future investment. Moreover, consideration of future opportunities is, for Brown, a key feature of human capital.

There was one common feature, however, of play development that seemed to resist the presentation of work ethic and flexibility. Playmakers discussed the ways in which they did not keep to time and often delayed or extended the development process. As noted in Section 3, at the Royal Shakespeare Company, Hill 'look[ed] for a main stage play to be developed over roughly two years', and, yet, in Arts Council England's (2009b) *Writ Large Report*, it was noted that playwrights rarely work to time in play development. For example: 'nearly all the theatres interviewed note a tendency for commissions not to be delivered on time (perhaps because – as has been mentioned – writers subsidise one under-paid project with another)' (90). Despite the clear need to develop a play within a time frame, all artists I interviewed seemed to have extended their time in play development for various reasons. Price's (2014) play development, for example, was extended because he independently decided to complete a higher than usual number of drafts: 'then I did loads and loads and loads of rewrites and then we went into rehearsals'. As Campbell, then the literary manager of the Royal Court, also observed, 'Tim Price, whose play is on now [*Teh Internet is Serious Business*, 2014] used to write a draft every week.'

For other artists, the lengthy duration of development was due to limitations in funding that extended the process. Zeldin (2017) noted that he 'had no money to do *Beyond Caring* [2014]. It was done in an unstructured way over a long period of time. [It was initially developed with The Yard]. The Yard Theatre were amazing in supporting the development'. Similarly, the development of RashDash's *We Want You to Watch* (2015) was extended due to limitations in seed-funding. Helen Goalen of RashDash (RashDash 2017) noted that, once Birch was on the team, they 'all went to see some work together in Germany. We went to "Find Festival" at The Schaubühne'. Greenland (RashDash 2017) added: 'no-one paid for us to go there. There was no bursary for tickets and flights. Before *We Want You to Watch* was funded by the National, RashDash had funded the early development itself.'

By decelerating play development, playmakers seemed to articulate parallels with the qualities of craftsmanship, passionate amateurism, and non-work defined by Harvie, Ridout, and Kunst. For example, craftsmanship, as noted, often implies inefficient use of time with periods of inactivity; passionate amateurism, for Ridout (2013), especially in a post-Fordist economy, is predicated on features including an attempt to 'interrupt the work-time rhythm ... and to produce precisely nothing' (99) and, furthermore, an emphasis on idle chatter and non-productive activity. Similarly, Kunst's conception of non-work as the presentation of 'laziness' and 'minimum effort' is central to the conception of the ways in which artists may resist their co-option by neoliberal subjectivity predominantly because, as Ridout notes so persuasively, such acts challenge the time disciplines of capitalism. In play development, we see that playmakers are keen to show that they haven't internalised the time disciplines of neoliberal subjectivity to the extent that they privilege economy and speed above the content and form of their commissioned work. Moreover, they do not seem to be forced, by themselves or theatres, to adopt the time disciplines of neoliberalism. For example, even though they have limited funding in early development, artists including Zeldin and RashDash do not seem to operate via economic principles that might have stipulated – for example, that a research trip to Germany for collaborators was unnecessary. As a result, by extending the development process, even before funding and a commission, artists seem to signal that play development operates outside the cost per benefit mentality of human capital.

Entrepreneurialism

By approaching play development with professionalism, responding to feedback, and, furthermore, maintaining strong business relations by praising their host theatres, playmakers demonstrate entrepreneurialism in play development. Playwrights demonstrate professionalism in responding to theatres' critiques and working practices. Porter (2014) sums this up as follows: 'I would say what I wanted to do with [the script] in conversation with Pippa [Hill] and Erica [Whyman]. Then Erica and Pippa would have discussions and feedback to me.' This process involved Porter demonstrating a high level of personal assurance in accepting feedback. This self-assurance is performed in the solitary writing and preparatory process. More-established playwrights responded to feedback without any evidence of emotional labour. For example, of feedback and rewriting, Price (2017) simply stated: 'then I did loads and loads and loads of rewrites and then we went into rehearsals'. Similarly, of his play *Crocodiles*, Mattinson (2017) said: 'The final week of rehearsal was with the Royal Exchange. They were coming in at this point and seeing runs and giving notes. Up until press night it was still getting changed.' Mattinson suggests here more pressure from the theatre. At the same time, however, it seems that, like Price, Mattinson reports a business-orientated approach in dealing with feedback. For less-established playmakers, however, the entrepreneurial performativity is oppressive. Matthews, for example, described his process as follows:

> They wanted me to prepare a draft for the director [Matthew Xia, who is now Associate Director at the Royal Exchange Theatre]. There were deadlines for me to hand the play to [Matthew]. . . . The draft that I handed in at that next deadline ended up being a lot worse. . . . The Everyman really did prepare me for it, but I don't think I [knew] how to prepare myself. It was [hard] because it was about airing my thoughts and feelings. I don't think I'd prepared myself for that.

Matthews' perception was that his new draft had become 'a lot worse'. It is unclear to what extent this opinion was shaped by the feedback he received, but that feedback was not read by Matthews as subjective; rather, he accepted it as the stipulated requests made by the service user for the service that Matthews was providing. Matthews thus attempted to respond in the most business-appropriate way possible, but his response demonstrates the artists' struggles as they appropriated the tenets of human capital in their dealings with theatres. Artists, however, showcased entrepreneurialism in praising the theatres they worked for, maintaining good business relations at all times. Price (2017) argued, for example, that the Royal Court 'is the most extraordinary writer-orientated space so they just said "whatever you need to get this done – we'll sort it"'. A similar sentiment was expressed by Zeldin (2017), who commented that 'I love working at the National. They're all so supportive. I'd received real resource and real support, technically, logistically but, also, morally [for *Beyond Caring* and, later, *Love*].' This positive reporting seems intimately connected to the playmakers' performance as human capital since there is a sense that business social relations govern the ways in which artists speak about their host theatres. Playmakers also performed with professionalism in enthusing about the process of play development. Agboluaje (2017) was able to, for instance, reconcile the potentially alienating aspects of his commission by outlining the social benefits of this experience because:

> It was exhausting, but it was really, really interesting. Rather than just write something and call it 'for young people', you realise when you meet a young person, when you've spoken to them, when you worked with them over a period, developing work together has a positive effect. It makes a difference.

By speaking passionately about the social relations of play development in these ways, playmakers demonstrate perhaps the most significant benefit in performing as human capitals in play development. By committing to a performance of entrepreneurialism that heightens the positive feedback they offer theatres and other artists, playmakers ensure their future success in the professional theatrical community, but also secure for others the same benefits. By endorsing each other and often being complicit in the commissioning of one another (e.g. Pirie with Price), artists invest in each other's human capital. The emphasis on sociality, however, could perhaps be read as an indication that artists are aligning with Ridout's (2013) passionate amateur who similarly strives for sociality and collaboration and simply passing the time together (136). In English play development, it is difficult to tell if a relationship is a friendship or one of mutual exchange around professional acumen. Crucially, because the focus here seems to be on mobilising sociality for productivity, the evidence suggests that, rather than resisting the terms of human capital, playmakers often acquiesce to them.

In interviews, however, artists often seemed to resist the terms of entrepreneurialism by emphasising how disorganised their relations with collaborators were and, furthermore, how sometimes the process led to failure rather than success. Rather than present their work as an entrepreneurial endeavour, for example, artists were keen to stress that their processes were determined by features similar to Kunst's emphasis on mistakes. Artists, for example, said they often made mistakes in their research phase. RashDash (2017) described how they had 'a splurge of all of that material on pornography that we were going through'. This 'splurge', which involved showcasing and discussing the resources they had collated, allowed them to make discoveries of how to move forward, using finds as devising material. It often, however, resulted in dead ends and changes in direction. Likewise, Mattinson (2017) described how he collated 'YouTube videos, pictures, bits of poems, bits of other plays' to find, again by a series of trial and error, material that would support the process. Mattinson's random acts of collection, which also led to dead ends, were informed by a desire to 'build up the feelings, and the tensions, of the play' – to find things that enabled a metalanguage around the project to emerge. Rather than read these deviations as resistant 'mistakes', however, these processes could be understood as aesthetic strategies to create an in-vogue commodity. Indeed, the emphasis on making mistakes and, more broadly, research and development in general is often observed as a central approach to entrepreneurial design, often aligning with, for example, traits including speculation and risk.

Overall, I suggest that, in play development in key English new writing theatres in the mid 2010s, artists in this sample were encouraged to conceive of themselves in paradigms of neoliberal subjectivity. By demonstrating brand marketability, work ethic, flexibility, and entrepreneurialism, it seems that artists' self-presentation is in line with that of human capital – as is mine in writing this Element, thus demonstrating my own brand marketability, work ethic, and flexibility in higher education. In play development, I suggest, playmakers are compelled to conceive of themselves as human capital and are thus awarded the prize of freedom in development – as per the neoliberal subjectivity paradigm. They perform the qualities of human capital to achieve this freedom which is experienced as artistic freedom. However, in line with the foregoing reading of neoliberal subjectivity, we can understand the freedom awarded in play development to be the payoff for the artists' self-investment and correlative to the extent to which the artist develops their brand marketability, work ethic, flexibility, and entrepreneurialism. I read the reframing of artists as units of human capital in play development as a complex evolution of creativity and creative labour during this period. As we have seen, neoliberal subject formation does benefit the individual artist (when successfully adopted). At the same time, it has resulted in additional labour for the artists. Overall, these sections have presented English play development as a hybrid activity that is not simply about playmaking, but also about business acumen, maintaining post-Fordist modes of production, and utilising a bureaucracy to enhance the functioning of English play development under neoliberalism.

Conclusion: Dreaming or Drowning? English Play Development Today

Wazobia: For centuries men have ruled ... mis-ruled us ...
The vandalism you saw a moment ago is only a minor
testimony of their era of misrule.
Time, blind like rain, knows no king.
Time has come for you to hear some home truths. (Tess Onwueme, *Wazobia Reigns*, 2016)

At the beginning of the play text for *Dreaming and Drowning* (2023), Owusu cites the opening of *Hamlet*: 'who's there?'. Taken more as a *crie de cœur* of the demos than the psychological terror of the ruling class, this statement channels a generation's feeling that it's time for some historical material home truths. 'Who's there' – in Shepard's Bush, in London, in English play development? In asking, Owusu becomes, as I see him, one of the luminaries strategising how to kill a zombie – the ghoulish (white) neoliberal pulse, in English play development, at the closing of its eerie and weird era. This Element began with a visit to the Lyric Hammersmith in 2014 and it ends with a visit to The Bush. On 23 December 2023, my partner and I went to a late-afternoon performance of *Dreaming and Drowning* after a morning spent at the Royal Academy's Marina Abramović retrospective. The day out was a significant expense in our budget. In 2023, the average Briton was nearly £2,000 worse off, while the average Londoner was nearly £3,400 worse off as a result of Brexit – with almost 300,000 fewer jobs in the capital alone (Mayor of London 2024). The retrospective, with an entirely white audience (during our time), was four times the price of Owusu's event, at which we were the only white spectators. But at both the Royal Academy and The Bush, visible signs of Christmas were minimal – for which we were grateful. The Bush was peaceful – despite the majority white Southampton away fans walking down the Uxbridge Road, howling in advance of a home match against Queens Park Rangers at the Loftus Road Stadium. Both myself and my partner had read the pre-show 'self-care' guide for Owusu's play – which focused on mental health issues including rising panic and anxiety. *Dreaming and Drowning* is dedicated to Owusu's mother, Naluwembe Binaisia, and, in a discussion on the writing of the play, Owusu cited Nigerian playwright Tess Onwueme's powerful 2016 *Wazobia Reigns* (see quotation at the beginning of this conclusion). *Wazobia Reigns* is a feminist drama that focuses on a gender reckoning and power transition which has significant impact on the role and place of women in the Anioma kingdom. By citing this text, Owusu's models of practice are aligned with the atmosphere of transitions of power. In this conclusion, I speak about *Dreaming and Drowning* at The Bush because I see it as a critical work of symbolic and direct action levelled against the spectre of neoliberal inequality outed as a feature of English play development, as noted in the introduction. In its address, *Dreaming and Drowning* invites its audience to answer 'who's there?' with their presence. As a diverse audience sitting quietly together in The Bush's modest studio space on a night before Christmas, we were there to witness what really matters in English play development now.

Dreaming and Drowning follows young, gifted, Black, and queer nineteen-year-old Malachi, who has just commenced a degree in English literature at the University of Bristol (though it is clear, as a former pretzel eater at the Westgate, he is from this area of London). The play begins with Malachi 'urgent and anxious' (2023, 7). He utters, 'I'm drownin. [space. Space]. Drowning under seas like heavy lava on my skin/ Melting my insides inside out *inside*/I'm falling fadin down into the damp/From open air to liquid blue, cold hue, where my lungs are/heavy, thick, I'm drownin/Drownin under blue and clutchin my throat fillin up upside *down*/ I'm turnin, blood rushin to my head/Legs like lead sinkin, thrashin gaspin' (7). 'I'm drowning' is a central reprise in the script, a metaphor of Malachi's anxiety – the result of the microaggression experienced in a white education system that privileges white, straight folks. It is, I suggest, also an allusion to Eric Garner's notorious last words, 'I can't breath', which became a *crie du cœur* of the Black Lives Matter movement. The focus on the body in *Dreaming and Drowning*, the repeated return to Malachi's increasingly severe panic attacks, forces a confrontation with the sympathetic nervous system. In each of Malachi's rising symptoms, we enter his fight-or-flight mode, experience through the allusion to the throat the respiratory system under strain, experience through the allusion to bloods the raised heartbeat, the increasing alertness and tension in muscle tissue, the digestive system shutdown, the sensory and perceptual disfigurements. The rhythm of his speech supports an understanding that this bodily response, however functional, has resulted in a very real danger to his maintaining homeostasis. In other words, if Malachi experiences himself drowning, it is because he is. And yet we watch.

The programming of Owusu's *Dreaming and Drowning* at The Bush enables its central institutional critique – Malachi's embodied response to a white institution – to reflect as much on English play development as on education. The Bush began in a small room above a pub on the corner of Shepherd's Bush Green in 1972. Since then, it has produced more than 500 groundbreaking premieres, becoming a world-famous new writing theatre while still retaining its aim to operate locally and 'reflect our culturally diverse area' (Bush Theatre 2025a). At the time of writing, the Bush had recently celebrated its fiftieth birthday (2022) cementing its reputation in producing new writing from playwrights 'from the widest range of backgrounds [who] who reflect the vibrancy of British culture now' (2025b). Its approach seems to work against the bureaucracy, modes of production, and artistic subjectivities of neoliberal English play development described in the earlier sections. Consider, for example, Benedict Lombe, a Congolese British writer whose debut play, *Lava*, received its world premiere at The Bush Theatre in 2021. Lombe notes:

> The Bush are my theatre family. I submitted a script during their open calls for script submissions and they invited me to join their Emerging Writers' group. This was an investment, in every sense of the word. From giving me the space to experiment and develop my craft – straight through to programming the world premiere of my debut play on their main stage. If you think it's just another scheme, think again. And then send in your play – they really are rooting for you (Bush Theatre 2025c).

Writers such as Benedict Lombe are not simply the recipients of The Bush's artistic management's 'rooting'; in turn, they root for others who engage with The Bush: their Black audiences. Following the death of George Floyd, The Bush released a YouTube series entitled 'The Protest: Black Lives Matter' (Bush Theatre 2025d). The description read: 'If we could we would have opened our building to support and comfort each other during this time. We would have held space together, cried together, and maybe made some art together in order to heal. ... Taking a second to speak directly to our Black audiences: we know that this is a difficult time.' Lombe's creative contribution, read emotionally to camera, begins: 'So as I try to write these words, I couldn't help but wonder about all those times in history when we've tried to write these words, about all these times in history where we've had to take our pain and our rage and our trauma and turn it into something articulate and insightful and poetic ... because this pain and this rage and this trauma is not articulate or insightful or poetic it's exhausting' (Bush Theatre 2025e). The departure of The Bush's management from managerial duties and the Bush's creatives from central commission duties during Black Lives Matter works against the imperatives of neoliberalism to present, instead, a model of relationality that is neither bureaucratic, Fordist, post-Fordist, nor expressive of neoliberal subjectivity.

The sensitivity and directness with which The Bush created content for its Black community in lockdown had ramifications for the address of its play development model which, during lockdown, was also issued as an open-access suite of videos on YouTube. The description for these videos, which remain available to anyone, reads: 'Since closing our doors, the Bush team has continued to work hard from home to bring exciting new voices to the UK stage. As part of this work, we are producing a short series of 10 Minute Masterclasses to support anyone who is interested in writing and plays.' Artistic Director Lynette Lindon and Director Dramaturg Daniel Bailey offer videos from their respective homes. In a masterclass exploring the difference between theme and story, Lindon is home, wearing a hoodie and no makeup. She has a fireplace just visible behind her – with a framed record on it. She commences with:

> I hope you're being gentle with yourselves. It's ok right now if you haven't written that full blown play that you planned to write during lockdown. It's ok if you haven't done all the reading you wanted to do. It's ok if all you're doing is watching RuPaul's *Drag Race* and eating loads of crisps – which is what I'm doing every Saturday. Whatever you're doing, and however you're coping: it's ok. And these videos exist to give you some tips when you're ready for those tips. That can be in a year's time from now – they're going to exist forever. Come back to this video whenever it is good for you. Ok? So today we're going to talk about the difference between theme and story and what to do when you're thinking about either. But before we do that I need a cup of tea so let's make one before we go for this ride! [story vs. theme slide].
>
> Lynette returns with a cup of tea in a Disney mug.

The register and tone of Lindon's introduction are markedly distinct from the often intimidating and white literature of playwriting pedagogy (see Tyler 2020). Furthermore, the proviso that the Bush's play development videos are 'going to exist forever' corresponds to Lombe's temporal claim that Black people throughout history have been solicited to provide the same insightful, articulate, and poetic responses of their pain. Lindon thus creates a subtle but significant rhetorical and address shift around the terms of English play development.

The subtext of Black creative legacy and ancestral connection is present not only in Lindon's and Lombe's discursive contributions, but also in the mode of expression of other creatives at The Bush, such as Daniel Bailey. In an interview with me in December 2022, Bailey described the function of the 'EWG' (Emerging Writers' Group) and the Bush's 'secret commitment that those plays end up on stage'. In articulating some wider thoughts on the industry now, Bailey said:

> We're looking cross-culturally at who's been able to tell stories. We're looking intergenerationally at who's been able to tell those stories and [seeking out] pieces that speak to each other across our programme. Do we have equality right now? I don't think so. And a lot of that is down to the leaders and gatekeepers of an industry which is sometimes struggling to keep completely relevant because of the ways of the world, and because of schools cutting their drama programmes. Our stories will always exist no matter how many schools disengage with drama and the arts. There's always going to be storytellers and people will always find their way. Our writers have always been writing stories and we've always had the stars to

look up to – to kind of revert to, and find your connection to the universe and the world. People are spiritual and we've always had the connection to look up to the stars. Suddenly, when the pandemic came, everything became a little more insular and insidious. And at this point, particularly in the UK and Ireland, we were, I hate to use this term, but we are quite confused about where we stood, about what we believed, and what we didn't. Storytellers always show us the best of ourselves and the worst of ourselves and, I think, writers at the time were writing very, very personal things with a lot of introspection because we had a lot of time on our hands. So that introspection has really informed the work we've had on. We've had so many monologue pieces because that was the zeitgeist because people spent so much time by themselves and were really asking questions about who they are and what they stood for. . . . *Lava* (Lombe) came out of the protest series which was a response to George Floyd. It was just visceral – we didn't try to contain it.

If attunement to Black legacy and ancestry are the conceptual underpinning of a new regime of play development at The Bush, this tenor is what supported writers such as Owusu. During the first lockdown in 2020, Owusu was a member of The Bush's emerging writers group (Campbell 2020). *Dreaming and Drowning*, Owusu's second play, was shortlisted for the Mustapha Matura award in 2022 (an award and mentoring programme for emerging and young Black playwrights of Caribbean and African descent, aged twenty-five and under). Ingrid Selberg, wife of Mustapha Matura, opines that 'I found Kwame Owusu's *Dreaming and Drowning* a powerful and authentic portrayal of a coming of age of a young Black person, which explored anxiety, anger, confusion and joy conveyed in vivid and poetic language. I feel Kwame Owusu is a writer with great promise and deserves to win the Mustapha Matura Award and Mentoring Programme' (Mustapha Matura 2025).

Represented here in both form and content is an experiential, phenomenological, and sensory account of the systematic oppression referenced in Lombe's critique of a play development model which 'take[s] our pain and our rage and our trauma and turn[s] it into something . . . poetic'. In the 2019–20 academic year, 72.6% of people starting undergraduate study were white, 12.2% were Asian, 8.7% were Black, 4.5% had mixed ethnicity, and 2.0% were from another ethnic group (Government UK 2022). As one of the 8.7%, Malachi is not unique but his rarefied presentation in higher education – and, rarer, the representation of campus plays – demonstrates a fervent rejection of hegemonies cited by Bailey as 'leaders and gatekeepers who are struggling to keep completely relevant'. Furthermore *Dreaming and Drowning* is a dramaturgical expression of Bailey's conviction that 'our stories will always exist no matter how many schools disengage with drama and the arts'. The drive that is created in uniting the rhetorical position of Lindon, Lombe, Bailey, and Owusu here creates a robust, future-oriented play development model that resists the neoliberal imperatives of bureaucracy, restructuring, and neoliberal subjectivity explored in earlier sections. So, now, as we enter the next phase of English play development: 'who's there?'.

References

Amin, A. (1996) *Post-Fordism: A Reader*, London: Blackwell.

Antonio, R. and Bonanno, A. (2000) 'A New Global Capitalism? From "Americanism and Fordism" to "Americanization-Globalization"', *American Studies*, Vol. 41, No. 2/3: 33–77.

Arts Council England (1989) *Towards Cultural Diversity*, London: Arts Council England.

(1997) *The Landscape of Fact: Towards a Policy for Cultural Diversity for the English Funding System*, London: Arts Council England.

(1998a) *Cultural Diversity Action Plan*, London: Arts Council England.

(1998b) *International Data on Public Spending in the Arts in Eleven Countries*, London: Arts Council England.

(2000a) [with Peter Boyden Associates] *Roles of the English Regional Producing Theatres Final Report*, London: Arts Council England.

(2000b) *The Next Stage: Towards a National Policy for Theatre in England*, London: Arts Council England.

(2000c) *National Policy for Theatre in England*, London: Arts Council England.

(2002a) *National Policy for Theatre in England*, London: Arts Council England.

(2002b) *Measuring the Economic and Social Impact of the Art*, London: Arts Council England.

(2003a) *Theatre Review*, London: Arts Council England.

(2003b) *Theatre Writing Strategy*, London: Arts Council England.

(2007) *Theatre Policy*, London: Arts Council England.

(2009a) *Theatre Assessment*, London: Arts Council England.

(2009b) *Writ Large: New Writing on the British Stage 2003–2009*, www.artscouncil.org.uk/sites/default/files/download-file/Writ_Large_New_Writing_on_the_English_Stage_2003-2009.pdf (accessed 6 October 2019).

(2009c) [with E. Dunton, R. Nelson, and H. Shand] *New Writing in Theatre 2003–08: An Assessment of New Writing within Smaller Scale Theatre in England*, www.artscouncil.org.uk/sites/default/files/download-file/New_writing_theatre_2003-8.pdf (accessed 06.10.19).

(2010) *Great Arts and Culture for Everyone*, http://withonevoice.com/sites/default/files/ACE%20Achieving%20Great%20Art%20for%20Everyone_0.pdf (accessed 06.10.19).

(2011a) *The Creative Case for Diversity*, www.artscouncil.org.uk/diversity/creative-case-diversity (accessed 06.10.19).

(2011b) *What Is the Creative Case for Diversity?*, www.creativecase.org.uk/domains/disabilityarts.org/local/media/audio/Final_What_is_the_Creative_Case_for_Diversity.pdf (accessed 06.10.19).

(2011c) *Supporting Growth in the Arts Economy*, www.a-n.co.uk/research/supporting-growth-arts-economy (accessed 06.10.19).

(2013) *Equality and Diversity within the Arts and Cultural Sector in England*, www.artscouncil.org.uk/sites/default/files/download-file/Equality_and_diversity_within_the_arts_and_cultural_sector_in_England.pdf (accessed 06.10.19).

(2014) *The Value of Arts and Culture to People and Society: An Evidence Review*, www.artscouncil.org.uk/sites/default/files/download-file/The_value_of_arts_and_culture_to_people_and_society_an_evidence_review.pdf (accessed 06.10.19).

(2015) [with P. Bazalgette] *Keynote. Diversity and the Creative Case: One Year On*, www.artscouncil.org.uk/sites/default/files/downloadfile/Keynote_Speech_Sir_Peter_Bazalgette_7_December_2015.pdf (accessed 06.10.19).

(2016) *Equality, Diversity and the Creative Case*, www.artscouncil.org.uk/sites/default/files/downloadfile/Equality_diversity_creativecase_2015_16_web_0.pdf (accessed 06.10.19).

(2017) *Analysis of Theatre in England*, www.artscouncil.org.uk/sites/default/files/downloadfile/Analysis%20of%20Theatre%20in%20England%20-%20Final%20Report.pdf (accessed 06.10.19).

(2018) *Equality, Diversity and the Creative Case*, www.artscouncil.org.uk/sites/default/files/downloadfile/Diversity_report_1617_FINAL_web.pdf (accessed 06.10.19).

Azunwo, E. E. (2014) 'Dramaturgy and Playwriting in the Theatre: Concepts of Conflicting Identity', published in the *CRAB Journal of Theatre and Media Arts*, Number 9/June 2014. Nigeria.

Baines, R., Marinetti, C., and Perteghella, M. (2011) *Staging and Performing Translation: Text and Theatre Practice*, Hampshire: Palgrave Macmillan.

Barbican Press (2021) 'Contributor D. D. Johnston', https://barbicanpress.com/contributor/d-d-johnston (accessed 16.02.25).

Bauman, Z. (2005) *Work, Consumerism and the New Poor*, Maidenhead: Open University Press.

BBC (2011) 'England Riots: 24-Hour Criminal Justice System after Riots', BBC News, www.bbc.co.uk/news/uk-england-14487636 (accessed 20.09.24).

Beech, M. (2015) 'The Ideology of the Coalition: More Liberal than Conservative' in Beech, M. and Lee, S. (eds.) *The Conservative Liberal Coalition: Examining the Cameron Clegg Government*, Basingstoke: Palgrave Macmillan, 1–15.

Berry, C. (2014) 'Quantity over Quality: A Political Economy of "Active Labour Market Policy" in the UK', *Policy Studies*, Vol. 35, No. 6: 592–610.

Bissel, L. and Weir, L. (eds.) (2022) *Performance in a Pandemic*, London: Routledge.

Boltanski, L. and Chiapello, E. (2018 [1999]) *The New Spirit of Capitalism*, London: Verso.

Bolton, J. (2008) 'Looking Back, Looking Forward: Literary Management at the Royal Court', *Contemporary Theatre Review*, Vol. 18, No. 1: 137–140.

—— (2011) 'Demarcating Dramaturgy: Mapping Theory onto Practice.' PhD diss., University of Leeds.

—— (2012) 'Capitalizing (on) New Writing: New Play Development in the 1990s', *Studies in Theatre and Performance*, Vol. 32, No. 2: 209–225.

Bourdieu, P. (1993) *The Field of Cultural Production*, Cambridge: Polity Press.

Bowerman, M., Raby, H., and Humphrey, C. (2000) 'In Search of the Audit Society: Some Evidence from Health Care, Police and Schools', *International Journal of Auditing*, Vol. 4, No. 1: 71–100.

Boyle, M. S. (2012) 'Revolution, Then and Now: Gob Squad's Sean Patten and Bastian Trost', *Theater*, Vol. 42, No. 3: 30–41.

—— (2017) 'Performance and Value: The Work of Theater in Karl Marx's Critique of Political Economy', *Theatre Survey*, Vol. 58, No. 1: 3–23.

Brown, W. (2015) *Undoing the Demos: Neoliberalism's Stealth Revolution*, New York: Zone Books.

—— (2019) *In the Ruins of Neoliberalism: The Rise of Antidemocratic Politics in the West*, New York: Columbia University Press.

Bury, P. and Catignani, S. (2019) 'Future Reserves 2020, the British Army and the Politics of Military Innovation during the Cameron Era', *International Affairs*, Vol. 95, No. 3: 681–701.

Bush Theatre (2025a) 'Vision for Our Local Work', www.bushtheatre.co.uk/community/our-strategy (accessed 16.02.25).

Bush Theatre (2025b) 'About Us', www.bushtheatre.co.uk/about-us (accessed 16.02.25).

Bush Theatre (2025c) 'Emerging Writers Group', www.bushtheatre.co.uk/artists/ewg (accessed 16.02.25).

Bush Theatre (2025d) 'The Protest: Black Lives Matter', www.youtube.com/watch?v=A99Hsd2Pgq0&list=PLM_bVvZ-NvDpQ1XX_wHQZzjtzQP-oFwmD (accessed 16.02.25).

Bush Theatre (2025e) '10 Minute Playwriting Masterclasses', https://www.you tube.com/watch?v=6ZN3qj7qgfQ (accessed 21.02.25).

Campbell, J. (2020) 'Autumn 2020 at the Bush Theatre', *The Voice*, 23 September, www.voice-online.co.uk/entertainment/arts-culture/2020/09/23/autumn-2020-at-the-bush-theatre.

Centre for Entrepreneurs (2014) 'The Entrepreneurs Manifesto', https://centreforentrepreneurs.org/wp-content/uploads/2015/11/CFE-Manifesto-Report.pdf (accessed 06.10.19).

Chandler, D. and Reid, J. (2016) *The Neoliberal Subject*, London: Rowman and Littlefield International.

Chandler, L. (2017) *Our Journey So Far*, www.youtube.com/watch?v=I1_BnSavv2o (accessed 06.10.19).

Clarke, J. (2010) 'After Neoliberalism?' *Cultural Studies*, Vol. 23, No. 3: 375–394.

Conroy, C. (2010) *Theatre and the Body*, Hampshire: Palgrave Macmillan.

— (2013) 'Paralympic Cultures: Disability as Paradigm', *Contemporary Theatre Review*, Vol. 23, No. 4: 519–531.

Cooper, D. (2004) *Challenging Diversity: Rethinking Equality and the Value of Difference*, Cambridge: Cambridge University Press.

Crossick, G. and Kaszynska, P. (2016) 'Understanding the Value of Arts and Culture: The AHRC Cultural Value Project', https://ahrc.ukri.org/documents/publications/cultural-value-project-final-report (accessed 06.10.19).

Diamond, E., Varney, D., and Amich, C. (eds.) (2017) *Performance, Feminism and Affect in Neoliberal Times*, Abingdon: Palgrave.

Dorey, P. (2007) 'A New Direction or Another False Dawn? David Cameron and the Crisis of British Conservatism', *British Politics*, Vol. 2, No. 2: 137–166.

— (2010) *British Conservatism: The Politics and Philosophy of Inequality*, London: IB Tauris.

— (2015) 'The Legacy of Thatcherism: Public Sector Reform' *Observatoire de la société britannique*, Vol. 17: 33–60.

Doustaly, C. and Gray C. (2010) 'Labour and the Arts: Managing Transformation?', *Observatoire de la société britannique*, Vol. 8: 319–338.

Dickson, A. (2009) 'The Drama Factory: How Theatre Scripts Reach the Stage'. The Guardian, 16 December. www.theguardian.com/stage/2009/dec/16/new-writing-theatre-slush-pile.

Edgar, D. (1999) 'State of Play: New Work in Contemporary British Theatre', *RSA Journal*, Vol. 141, No. 5440: 450–460.

— (2004) 'Where's the Challenge?' *The Guardian*, www.theguardian.com/artanddesign/2004/may/22/artspolicy (accessed 06.10.19).

(2013) 'Playwriting Studies: Twenty Years On', *Contemporary Theatre Review*, Vol. 23, No. 2: 99–106.

(2015) 'The Playwright's Still the Thing', *The Guardian*, www.theguardian.com/commentisfree/2015/jan/29/playwright-death-british-dramatist-exaggerated-surge-new-plays (accessed 06.10.19).

Equality Act (2010) www.legislation.gov.uk/ukpga/2010/15/contents (accessed 06.10.19)

Equality Act Guidance (2015) www.gov.uk/guidance/equality-act-2010-guidance (accessed 06.10.19)

Elliott-Cooper, A. *Black Resistance to British Policing*, Manchester: Manchester University Press.

Emenike-Azunwo, E. (2020) 'Playwriting: An Analysis of the Morphological Characteristics of Whatsapp and Facebook Messages', *Acta Universitatis Danubius. Communicatio* 14.1.

Firebird Theatre (2007) 'Faustus Tour 2007 Project Evaluation', www.firebird-theatre.com/resources/Firebird%20evaluation%204.pdf (accessed 06.10.19).

Fisher, M. (2009) *Capitalist Realism: Is There No Alternative?* Hants: Zero Books.

Fisher, M. and Gilbert, J. (2016 [2013]) 'Capitalist Realism and Neoliberal Hegemony: A Dialogue' in Gilbert, J. (ed.) *Neoliberal Culture*, London: Lawrence and Wishart: 124–141.

Fisher, T. and Gotman, K. (2020) *Foucault's Theatres*, Manchester, Manchester University Press.

Foucault, M. (2008) *The Birth of Biopolitics: Lectures at the College de France, 1978–1979*, trans. Graham Burchell, Hampshire: Palgrave Macmillan.

Frayling, C. (2005) *The Only Trustworthy Book: Arts and Public Value*, London: Arts Council England.

Freeman, S. (2017) 'New Writing and Theatre History', *Theatre History Studies*, Vol. 36: 115–126.

Gardner, L. (2006) 'Where Are All the Good New Playwrights?', *The Guardian*, www.theguardian.com/stage/theatreblog/2006/oct/30/frompagetostage (accessed 06.10.19).

Gilbert, J. (ed.) (2016 [2015]) *Neoliberal Culture*, London: Lawrence and Wishart.

Gilbert, J. (2016 [2013]) 'What Kind of Thing Is Neoliberalism' in Gilbert, J. (ed.) *Neoliberal Culture*, London: Lawrence and Wishart, 10–33.

Gilroy, P. (2016 [2013]) '"... We Got to Get Over Before We Go Under ..." Fragments for a History of Black Vernacular Neoliberalism' in Gilbert, J. (ed.) *Neoliberal Culture*, London: Lawrence and Wishart, 33–55.

Giroux, H. A. (2014) *Neoliberalism's War on Higher Education*, Chicago, IL: Haymarket Books.

Goldman, P. and Van Houten, D. R (1977) 'Managerial Strategies and the Worker: A Marxist Analysis of Bureaucracy', *Sociological Quarterly*, Vol. 18, No. 1: 108–125.

Government UK (2022) 'First Year Entrants onto University Study', https://www.ethnicity-facts-figures.service.gov.uk/education-skills-and-training/higher-education/first-year-entrants-onto-undergraduate-degrees/latest/#:~:text=72.6%25%20of%20people%20starting%20undergraduate,from%20the%20Other%20ethnic%20group (accessed 22.02.25).

Graeber, D. (2016 [2015]) *The Utopia of Rules: On Technology, Stupidity and the Secret Joys of Bureaucracy*, New York: Melville House.

Gramsci, A. (1999 [1926]) *Selections from the Prison Notebooks*, London: Elecbook.

Gray, C. (2004) 'Joining-Up or Tagging On? The Arts, Cultural Planning and the View from Below', *Public Policy and Administration*, Vol. 19, No. 2: 38–49.

Hall, S. (1988) 'Brave New World', *Marxism Today*: 24–29. http://banmarchive.org.uk/collections/mt/pdf/88_10_24.pdf (accessed 06.10.19).

(2011) 'The Neoliberal Revolution: Thatcher, Blair, Cameron – the Long March of Neoliberalism Continues', *Soundings*, Vol. 48: 9–27.

Hardt, M. and Negri, A. (2001) *Empire*, Cambridge, MA: Harvard University Press.

Hargrave, M. (2015) *Theatres of Learning Disability*, Hampshire: Palgrave Macmillan.

Harvey, D. (1990) 'Between Space and Time: Reflections on the Geographical Imagination', *Annals, Association of American Geographers*, Vol. 80, No. 3 418–434.

(2005) *A Brief history of Neoliberalism*, Oxford: Oxford University Press.

(2006) *Spaces of Global Capitalism: Towards a Theory of Uneven Geographical Development*, London: Verso.

(2010) *A Companion to Marx's Capital*, London: Verso.

Harvie, J. (2005) *Staging the UK*, Manchester: Manchester University Press.

(2013) *Fair Play: Art, Performance and Neoliberalism*, London: Palgrave Macmillan.

(2015) 'Funding, Philanthropy, Structural Inequality and Decline in England's Theatre Ecology', *Cultural Trends*, Vol. 24, No. 1: 56–61.

Haslett, R. (2011) 'Architecture and New Play Development at The National Theatre, 1907–2010', *New Theatre Quarterly*, Vol. 24, No. 4: 358–367.

Hay, C. (2018) 'Brexit and the Multiple Paradoxes of Neoliberalism', https://sase.org/wp-content/uploads/2018/04/1-Hay-final.pdf (accessed 20.04.24)

Hayton, R. and McEnhill, L. (2015) 'Cameron's Conservative Party, Social Liberalism and Social Justice', *British Politics*, Vol. 10, No. 2: 131–147.

Healy, S. (2022) *The Literary Manager's Toolkit: A Practical Guide for the Theatre*. London: Routledge.

Heddon, D. and Milling, J. (2006) *Devising Performance*, Basingstoke: Palgrave Macmillan.

Hesmondhalgh, D., Nisbett, M., Oakley, K., and Lee, D. (2014) 'Were New Labour's Cultural Policies Neo-Liberal?, *International Journal of Cultural Policy*, Vol. 21, No. 1: 97–114.

Hewison, R. (1997 [1995]) *Culture and Consensus: England, Arts and Politics since 1940*, Oxon: Routledge.

——— (2014) *Cultural Capital: The Rise and Fall of Creative Britain*, London, Verso.

Hirst, P. (1995) 'Quangos and Democratic Government', *Political Affairs*, Vol. 48, No. 2: 341–359.

HM Treasury (2002) *Spending Review: Department Investment Strategies*. https://webarchive.nationalarchives.gov.uk/20071204181456/, http://www.hm-treasury.gov.uk/media/9/B/dis_whitepaper02.pdf (accessed 06.10.19).

Holden, J. (2004). *Capturing Cultural Value: How Culture Has Become a Tool of Government Policy*, London: Demos.

Holden, N. (2017) 'Making New Theatre Together: The First Writers' Group and the Royal Court Theatre and Its Legacy within the Young Writers' Programme', *Theatre History Studies*, Vol. 36: 248–265.

Hood, C. (1991) 'A Public Management for All Seasons?', *Public Administration*, Vol. 69, No. 1: 3–19.

——— (1995) 'The 'New Public Management' in the 1980s: Variations on a Theme', *Accounting, Organizations and Society*, Vol. 20, No. 2–3: 93–109.

Hunter, A. (2016) 'The Changing Faces of Fordism: The Nature of Service Work Today' Leeds Metropolitan University, School of Social, Psychological and Communication Sciences (download).

Inchley, M. (2015) *Voice and New Writing, 1997–2007: Articulating the Demos*, London: Palgrave Macmillan.

Independent Theatre Council (ITC) (2005) 'Capturing the Audience Experience: A Handbook for the Theatre'. https://itc-arts-s3.studiocoucou.com/uploads/helpsheet_attachment/file/23/Theatre_handbook.pdf (accessed 06.10.19)

James, O. (2004) 'The UK Core Executive's Use of Public Service Agreements as a Tool of Governance', *Public Administration*, Vol. 82, No. 2: 397–419.

Jessop, B. (1989) 'Conservative Regimes and the Transition to Post-Fordism: The Cases of Great Britain and West Germany' in Gottdiener, M. and Komninos, N (eds.) *Capitalist Development and Crisis Theory: Accumulation, Regulation, and Spatial Restructuring*, Basingstoke: Macmillan: 261–299.

(1992) 'Fordism and Post-Fordism: A Critical Reformulation' in Scott, A. J and Storper, M. J. *Pathways to Regionalism and Industrial Development*, London: Routledge, 43–65.

(2018) 'Neoliberalization, Uneven Development, and Brexit: Further Reflections on the Organic Crisis of the British State and Society', *European Planning Studies*, Vol. 26, No. 9: 1728–1746.

Jowell, T. (2004) *Government and the Value of Culture*. https://shiftyparadigms.files.wordpress.com/2015/08/tessa_jowell.pdf (accessed 06.10.19).

Kennedy, F. (2009) 'Why Adopting Playwrights Is No Laughing Matter', *The Guardian*, www.theguardian.com/stage/theatreblog/2009/may/04/adopt-playwright (accessed 06.10.19).

Kennedy, F. and Campbell Pickford, H. (2013) *In Battalions: A Snap-Shot of New Play Development at the Start of 2013*, www.researchgate.net/publication/321334265_In_Battalions_A_Snapshot_of_new_play_development_in_England_2013 (accessed 06.10.19).

(2014) *In Battalions Delphi Study*, www.scribd.com/document/203083584/In-Battalions-Delphi-Study (accessed 06.10.19).

Kundnani, A. (2021) 'The Racial Constitutions of Neoliberalism', *Institute of Race Relations*, Vol. 63, No. 1: 51–69.

Kunst, B. (2012) 'Art and Labour: On Consumption, Laziness and Less Work', *Performance Research*, Vol. 17, No. 6: 116–125.

(2015) *Artist at Work, Proximity of Art and Capitalism*, Winchester: Zero Books.

La Berge, L, C. (2019) *Wages against Artwork: Decommodified Labor and the Claims of Socially Engaged Art*, Durham, NC: Duke University Press.

Lacey, S. (2004) 'British Theatre and Commerce, 1979–2000' in Kershaw, B. (ed.) *Cambridge History of British Theatre*, Volume 3, Cambridge: Cambridge University Press, 426–447.

Lapsley, I. (2009) 'New Public Management: The Cruellest Invention of the Human Spirit?', *Abacus*, Vol. 45, No. 1: 1–21.

Lazzarato, M. (1996) 'Immaterial Labor', in *Radical Thought in Italy: A Potential Politics*, eds. by Virno, P. and Hardt, M., Minneapolis: University of Minnesota Press: 133–147.

Lentin, A. and Titley, G. (2011) *The Crisis of Multiculturalism: Racism in a Neoliberal Age*, Croydon: Zed Books.

Lesage, D. (2012). 'Permanent Performance'. *Performance Research*, Vol. 17, No. 6: 14–21. https://doi.org/10.1080/13528165.2013.775752.

Lewchuk, W. (1989) 'Fordist Technology and Britain: The Diffusion of Labour Speed Up', A paper presented at the Warwick Economics Summer

Workshop, https://warwick.ac.uk/fac/soc/economics/research/workingpapers/1989-1994/twerp340.pdf (accessed 06.10.19).

Love, C. (2015) 'A Culture of Development: The Royal Court and the Young Writers' Programme', *Society for Theatre Research*, Vol. 69, No. 2: 113–123.

(2016a) 'New Perspectives on Home: Simon Stephens and Authorship in British Theatre', *Contemporary Theatre Review*, Vol. 23, No. 3: 319–327.

(2016b) 'By the Book: Adaptation, Work and Elevator Repair Service's Gatz', *Contemporary Theatre Review*, Vol. 26, No. 2: 183–195.

Luckhurst, M. (2006) *Dramaturgy: A Revolution in Theatre*, Cambridge, Cambridge University Press.

(2010) 'Dramaturgy and Agendas of Change: Tinderbox and the Joint Sectoral Dramaturgy Project', *Contemporary Theatre Review*, Vol. 20, No. 2: 173–184.

MacDonald, C. (2010) 'Conducting the Flow: Dramaturgy and Writing', *Studies in Theatre and Performance*, Vol. 30, No. 1: 91–100.

Marx, K. (1977 [1859]) *A Contribution to the Critique of Political Economy*, notes by R. Rojas, Moscow: Progress.

(1973 [1861]) *Grundrisse: Foundations of the Critique of Political Economy*, trans. Martin Nicolaus, New York: Penguin.

(1990 [1867]) *Capital Volume One*, trans., Ben Fowkes, St Ives: Penguin Books.

(2009 [1843]) *Critique of Hegel's Philosophy of Right*, trans., Annette Jolin and Joseph O'Malley, Cambridge University Press Digital edition.

(2015 [1859]) *A Contribution to the Critique of Political Economy*, trans., N. I Stone, New York, kindle edition, Palala Press.

Marx, K. and Engels, F. (2000[1845–6]) *The German Ideology: Parts I and II*, Moscow, Progress.

Matthews, A. E. (2017) 'Giving Service and Provoking Rupture: The Post-Fordist Performer at Work', *Studies in Theatre and Performance*, Vol. 37, No. 1: 139–154.

Mayor of London (2024) 'Mayor Highlights Brexit Damage to London Economy', www.london.gov.uk/new-report-reveals-uk-economy-almost-ps140billion-smaller-because-brexit#:~:text=The%20average%20Briton%20was%20nearly,jobs%20in%20the%20capital%20alone (accessed 20.10.24).

McCarthy, K, F. et al. (2004) *Gifts of the Muse: Reframing the Debate about the Benefits of the Arts*, www.rand.org/content/dam/rand/pubs/monographs/2005/RAND_MG218.pdf (accessed 07.10.19).

References

McDowell, L. (2009) *Working Bodies: Interactive Service Employment and Workplace Identities*, Chichester: Wiley-Blackwell.

McEvoy, W. and McHugh, I. (2016) 'Rewriting the Script: The Impact of the Development and Rehearsal Process on Ian McHugh's Play How to Curse', *Contemporary Theatre Review*, Vol. 26, No. 4: 496–505.

McGuigan, J. (2005) 'Neo-liberalism, Culture and Policy', *International Journal of Cultural Policy*, Vol. 11, No. 3: 229–241.

The McMaster Review (2008), Culture Tourism and Sport Board, http://lga.moderngov.co.uk/Data/Culture,%20Tourism%20&%20Sport%20Board/20080529/Agenda/$Item%203%20-%20McMaster.doc.pdf (accessed 07.10.19)

Merton, R. K. (1957) *Social Theory and Social Structure*. Glencoe, IL, The Free Press.

Meyrick, J. (2006) 'Cut and Paste: The Nature of Dramaturgical Development in Theatre', *Theatre Research International*, Vol. 31, No. 3: 270–282.

Miller, H. (2013) 'Advice to Applicants: Labor, Value, and MFA Program Design', *A Journal of Performance and Art*, Vol. 35, No. 1: 32–42.

Mirowski, P. (2013) *Never Let a Serious Crisis Go to Waste: How Neoliberalism Survived the Financial Meltdown*, New York: Verso.

Mustapha Matura (2025) 'Award and Mentoring Programme', https://mustaphamatura.com/the-mustapha-matura-award (accessed 16.02.25).

Mylonas, Y. (2011) 'Amateur Creation and Entrepreneurialism: A Critical Study of Artistic Production in Post-Fordist Structures', *TripleC*, Vol. 10, No. 1: 1–11.

The National Theatre, 'New Work Department', www.nationaltheatre.org.uk/about-the-national-theatre/new-work (accessed 07.10.19).

Negri, A. (2017) *Marx and Foucault*, trans. Emery E., Cambridge: Polity Press.

New Economics Foundation (NEF) (2008) 'Well-Being Analysis', London: New Economics Foundation.

Nielson, L, D. and Ybarra, P. (eds.) (2015 [2012]) *Neoliberalism and Global Theatres*, Hampshire, Palgrave Macmillan.

Onwueme, T. (2016) *Wazobia Reigns*. USA: International Images Net.

Peck, J. (2013) 'Explaining (with) Neoliberalism', *Territory, Politics, Governance*, Vol. 1, No. 2: 132–157.

Peck, J. and Theodore, N. (2012) 'Reanimating Neoliberalism: Process Geographies of Neoliberalization', *Social Anthropology/Anthropologie Sociale*, Vol. 20, No. 2: 177–185.

Pinchbeck, M. (2016) *Acts of Dramaturgy: The Dramaturgical Turn in Contemporary Performances* (2016) PhD diss., University of Loughborough.

Previtali, F. S. and Fagiani, C. C. (2015) 'Deskilling and Degradation of Labour in Contemporary Capitalism: The Continuing Relevance of Braverman', *Work Organisation, Labour & Globalisation*, Vol. 9, No. 1: 76–91.

Radosavljević, D. (2009) The Need to Keep Moving, *Performance Research*, Vol. 14, No. 3: 45–51.

(2013a) *Theatre-Making: Interplay between Text and Performance in the 21st Century*, Hampshire: Palgrave Macmillan.

(2013b) *The Contemporary Ensemble: Interviews with Theatre-Makers*, Oxon: Routledge.

Ratcliffe, P. (2004) *Race, Ethnicity and Difference: Imagining the Inclusive Society*, Maidenhead: Open University Press.

Read, J. (2009) 'A Genealogy of Homo-Economicus: Neoliberalism and the Production of Subjectivity', *Foucault Studies*, No. 6: 25–36.

Rebellato, D. (2006) 'Playwriting and Globalisation: Towards a Site-Unspecific Theatre', *Contemporary Theatre Review*, Vol. 16, No. 1: 97–113.

(2009) *Theatre and Globalization*, Hampshire: Macmillan.

Reeves, M. (2002) *Measuring the Economic and Social Impact of the Arts*, London: Arts Council England.

Rhodes, C. (2020) 'Manufacturing: Statistics and Policy', House of Commons Briefing Paper, 10 January. https://commonslibrary.parliament.uk/research-briefings/sn01942.

Ridout, N. (2013) *Passionate Amateurs: Theatre, Communism, and Love*, Kindle edition: University of Michigan Press.

Ritzer, G. (1996) *The McDonalidization of Society*, London: Sage.

Robinson, R. C. (2012) 'Funding the "Nation" in the National Theatre of Scotland', *International Journal of Cultural Policy*, Vol.18, No.1: 46–58.

Romanska, M. (ed.) (2014) *Routledge Companion to Dramaturgy*, Oxon: Routledge.

Rumbold, K. (2008) 'Policy Review: The Art Council England's "Arts Debate"', *Cultural Trends*, Vol. 17, No. 3: 189–195.

Rustin, M. (1989) 'The Politics of Post-Fordism, or the trouble with "New Times"', *New Left Review*, Vol. 1, No. 75. https://newleftreview.org/issues/i175/articles/michael-rustin-the-politics-of-post-fordism-or-the-trouble-with-new-times (accessed 16.02.25).

Sanandaji, N. (2014) 'Entrepreneurs Power the Best Economies', *The Telegraph*, www.telegraph.co.uk/news/politics/10791836/Entrepreneurs-power-the-best-economies.html (accessed 07.10.19).

Schmidt, T. (2013) 'Troublesome Professionals: On the Speculative Reality of Theatrical Labour', *Performance Research*, 18:2: 15–26.

Schmitt, J. and Jones, J. (2013) 'Slow Progress for Fast Food Workers', *Centre for Economic and Policy Researchers*, https://cepr.net/documents/publications/fast-food-workers-2013-08.pdf (accessed 07.10.19).

Schneider, R. (2011) *Performing Remains: Art and War in Times of Theatrical Reenactment*, Oxon: Routledge.

Selwood, S. (2002) 'The Politics of Data Collection: Gathering, Analysing and Using Data about the Subsidised Cultural Sector in England', *Cultural Trends*, Vol. 12, No. 47: 13–84.

Shellard, D. (2004) *Economic Impact Study of UK Theatre*, https://webarchive.nationalarchives.gov.uk/20160204123942/, http://www.artscouncil.org.uk/advice-and-guidance/browse-advice-and-guidance/economic-impact-study-of-uk-theatre (accessed 07.10.19).

Sh!t Theatre (2018) *DollyWould*. London: Bloomsbury.

Sierz, A. (2008) 'Tim Fountain: Playwriting and Sex, Sex, Sex', *Theatre Voice*, www.theatrevoice.com/audio/tim-fountain-playwriting-and-sex/ (accessed 07.10.19).

—— (2011) *Rewriting the Nation: British Theatre Today*, London: Methuen Drama.

Six, T. (2024) 'Performing Counterinsurgency: *Death of England* and the Racial Regime', https://static1.squarespace.com/static/6271069da3a0ad749c9a153a/t/66753fc0d2dda56ab711aeaa/1718960064924/Tom+Six%2C+Performing+Counterinsurgency+Paper+June+24.pdf.

Slobodian, Q. (2018) *Globalists: The End of Empire and the Birth of Neoliberalism*, Cambridge, MA: Harvard University Press.

Solga, K. (2019) *Theatre and Performance in the Neoliberal University: Responses to an Academy in Crisis*, Abingdon: Palgrave.

Squire, V. (2005) 'Integration with Diversity in Modern Britain' : New Labour on Nationality, Immigration and Asylum', *Journal of Political Ideologies*, Vol. 10, No.1: 51–74.

Stone, K. (1973) 'The Origins of Job Structures in the Steel Industry', *Radical America*, Vol. 7: 17–66.

Tomlin, L. (2013a) '"Make a Map Not a Tracing": From Pedagogy to Dramaturgy', *Contemporary Theatre Review*, Vol. 23, No. 2: 120–127.

—— (2013b) 'Foreword' in Angelaki, V. (ed.) *Contemporary British Theatre: Breaking New Ground*, Hampshire: Palgrave Macmillan: loc. 53–499.

—— (2013c) *Acts and Apparitions: Discourses on the Real in Performance Practice and Theory, 1990–2010*, Manchester: Manchester University Press.

—— (2014) *British Theatre Companies 1995–2014*, London: Bloomsbury.

(2016) 'From Text to New Writing: Interrogating the "New" in England's New Writing Narrative' *British Theatre in the 21st Century: New Texts, New Stages, New Identities, New Worlds*, Paris-Sorbonne et Ecole Normale Supérieure, 13.10.2016-15.10.2016.

(et al.) (2017) *Incubate: Propagate. Networked Ecologies of New Performance Making*, http://eprints.gla.ac.uk/151581/1/151581.pdf (accessed 07.10.19).

(ed.) (forthcoming) 'Artist Development: Class, Diversity and Exclusion', *Studies in Theatre and Performance*, Vol. 40.

Trencsényi, K. and Cochrane, B. (eds.) (2014) *New Dramaturgy: International Perspectives on Theory and Practice*, London: Methuen.

Trencsényi, K. (2015) *Dramaturgy in the Making: A Guide for Practitioners*, Suffolk: Methuen.

Trottier, D. (2014 [1994]) *Screenwriter's Bible*, Hollywood, CA: Silman-James Press.

Trueman, M. (2019) 'Alan Ayckbourn at 80', *The Guardian*. www.theguardian.com/stage/2019/apr/12/alan-ayckbourn-80th-birthday-penelope-wilton-ben-miles-nina-sosanya (accessed 07.10.19).

Turner, C. (2009) 'Getting the 'Now' into the Written Text (and Vice Versa): Developing Dramaturgies of Process' *Performance Research*, Vol. 14, No. 1: 106–114.

(2013) 'Learning to Write Spaces', *Contemporary Theatre Review*, Vol. 23, No. 2: 114–119.

Turner, C. and Behrndt, S. (2008) *Dramaturgy and Performance*. Basingstoke: Palgrave.

(2010) 'Editorial', *Contemporary Theatre Review*, Vol. 20, No. 2: 145–148.

Tyler, L. (2017) '"Responding to the Thing That It Is": A Study of New Play Development in English Theatres', *Studies in Theatre and Performance*, published online, http://dx.doi.org/10.1080/14682761.2017.1348682 (accessed 07.10.19).

(2020) '"Almost, but Not Quite": Reading Debbie Tucker Green's Dramaturgy inside British Playwriting Studies', in Adiseshiah, S. and Bolton, J. (eds.) *Debbie Tucker Green: Critical Perspectives*, Palgrave Macmillan, 129–150.

Virno, P. (2004) *A Grammar of the Multitude: For an Analysis of Contemporary Forms of Life*, Los Angeles, CA: Semiotext(e).

(2009) 'The Dismeasure of Art', in Geilan, P. and de Bruyne, P. (eds.), *Being an Artistic in Post-Fordist Times*, New York: Distributed Art Publishers.

Weber, M. (1978 [1968]) *Economy and Society: An Outline of Interpretive Sociology*, Rother, G. and Wittich, C. (eds.) Berkeley: University of California Press.

Wiggan, J. (2015) 'Reading Active Labour Market Policy Politically: An Autonomist Analysis of Britain's Work Programme and Mandatory Work Activity', *Critical Social Policy*, Vol. 35, No. 3: 369–392.

Willis, P. (2017 [1977]) *Learning to Labour: How Working Class Kids Get Working Class Jobs*, New York: Columbia University Press.

Win, T. S. (2014) 'Marketing the Entrepreneurial Artists in the Innovation Age: Aesthetic Labor, Artistic Subjectivity, and the Creative Industries', *Anthropology of Work Review*, Vol. 35, No. 1: 2–13.

The Writers' Guild (2012) *The Working Playwright Engaging with Theatres*, https://writersguild.org.uk/wpcontent/uploads/2015/02/WGGB_booklet_nov12_engaging_i.pdf (accessed 07.10.19).

   (2015) *Agreements and Contracts: A Working Writers' Guide*. https://writersguild.org.uk/wpcontent/uploads/2015/02/Agreements-and-Contracts-2016.1.pdf (accessed 07.10.19).

Ybarra, P.A. (2017) *Latinx Theater in the Times of Neoliberalism*, Evanston, IL: Northwestern University Press.

Unpublished Interviews

Agboluaje, O. (2017) Playwright commissioned by Plymouth Drum Theatre, unpublished interview with Tyler. 28 June.

Bell, S. (2014) New Writing Associate and Dramaturg at Royal Exchange Theatre, unpublished interview with Tyler. 18 September.

Camden, S. (2017) Spoken word artist commissioned by Birmingham Rep, unpublished interview with Tyler. 10 July.

Campbell, C. (2014) Literary Manager of the Royal Court, unpublished interview with Tyler. 30 September.

Casement, T. (2014) Associate Director of Mercury Theatre, unpublished interview with Tyler. 29 August.

Greggs, H. (2014) Literary Associate at the Liverpool Everyman and Playhouse, unpublished interview with Tyler. 4 November.

Hill, P. (2014) Literary Manager at Royal Shakespeare Company, unpublished interview with Tyler. 23 September.

Lyons, T. (2015) New Writing Associate and Dramaturg at the National Theatre, unpublished interview with Tyler. 12 May.

Matthews, D. (2017) Playwright commissioned by the Liverpool Everyman and Playhouse, unpublished interview with Tyler. 4 June.

Mattinson, L. (2017) Playwright commissioned by Royal Exchange Theatre, unpublished interview with Tyler. 11 July.

Pawson, J. (2014) Young Peoples' Producer at Plymouth Drum, unpublished interview with Tyler. 10 September.

Porter, P. (2014) Playwright commissioned by Royal Shakespeare Company, unpublished interview with Tyler. 12 November.

Price, T. (2017) Playwright commissioned by the Royal Court, unpublished interview with Tyler. 3 July.

RashDash (2017) Associate Theatre Company of West Yorkshire Playhouse, unpublished interview from Greenland, A. and Goalan, H. with Tyler. 26 July.

Rosenblatt, M. (2014) Associate Director at the West Yorkshire Playhouse, unpublished interview with Tyler. 12 September.

Smith, A. (2017) Playwright of *Summit*, unpublished interview with Tyler. 12 April.

Walker, T. (2015) Associate Director at Birmingham Repertory Theatre, unpublished interview with Tyler. 5 March.

Whittington, A. (2017) Playwright commissioned by Mercury Theatre, unpublished interview with Tyler. 21 July.

Wohead, G. (2018) Playmaker of *Call It a Day*, unpublished interview with Tyler. 19 November.

Zeldin, A. (2017) Playmaker commissioned by The National Theatre, unpublished interview with Tyler. 29 June.

About the Author

Lucy Tyler is an associate professor of performance at the University of Reading. She is an artist and dramaturg. Lucy has supported new writing since 2010. Her practice expanded until she was co-creating with diverse companies in the UK, Europe, the USA, and Brazil. Her research explores what it is to be with artists as they make. Lucy leads an Arts Council England-funded project in conjunction with South Street Arts Centre, Reading, UK. The project, entitled 'Work in Progress', seed-funds and facilitates the development of new touring performances by emerging and mid-stage career artists of national and international acclaim.

Cambridge Elements⸗

Contemporary Performance Texts

Senior Editor
Fintan Walsh
Birkbeck, University of London
Fintan Walsh is Professor of Performing Arts and Humanities at Birkbeck, University of London, where he is Head of the School of Creative Arts, Culture and Communication and Director of Birkbeck Centre for Contemporary Theatre. He is a former Senior Editor of *Theatre Research International*.

Associate Editors
Duška Radosavljević
Royal Central School of Speech and Drama, University of London
Duška Radosavljević is a Professorial Research Fellow at the Royal Central School of Speech and Drama. Her work has received the David Bradby Research Prize (2015), the Elliott Hayes Award for Dramaturgy (2022) and the ATHE-ASTR Award for Digital Scholarship.

Caridad Svich
Rutgers University
Caridad Svich is a playwright and translator. She teaches creative writing and playwriting in the English Department at Rutgers University-New Brunswick.

Advisory Board
Siân Adiseshiah, *Loughborough University*
Helena Grehan, *Murdoch University*
Ameet Parameswaran, *Jawaharlal Nehru University*
Synne Behrndt, *Stockholm University of the Arts*
Jay Pather, *University of Cape Town*
Sodja Zupanc Lotker, *The Academy of Performing Arts in Prague (DAMU)*
Peter M. Boenisch, *Aarhus University*
Hayato Kosuge, *Keio University*
Edward Ziter, *NYU Tisch School of the Arts*
Milena Gras Kleiner, *Pontificia Universidad Católica de Chile*
Savas Patsalidis, *Aristotle University, Thessaloniki, Greece*
Harvey Young, *College of Fine Arts, Boston University*

About the Series
Contemporary Performance Texts responds to the evolution of the form, role and meaning of text in theatre and performance in the late twentieth and twenty-first centuries, by publishing Elements that explore the generation of text for performance, its uses in performance, and its varied modes of reception and documentation.

Cambridge Elements⹀

Contemporary Performance Texts

Elements in the Series

Playwriting, Dramaturgy and Space
Sara Freeman

Performing Grief in Pandemic Theatres
Fintan Walsh

Theatricality, Playtexts and Society
David Barnett

The Poetics of Performance Diagrams
Andrej Mirčev

Comedy and Controversy: Scripting Public Speech
Sarah Balkin and Marc Mierowsky

English Play Development under Neoliberalism, 2000–2022
Lucy Tyler

A full series listing is available at: www.cambridge.org/ECTX

For EU product safety concerns, contact us at Calle de José Abascal, 56–1°, 28003 Madrid, Spain or eugpsr@cambridge.org.

www.ingramcontent.com/pod-product-compliance
Lightning Source LLC
LaVergne TN
LVHW022040260326
834688LV00061B/1664